COSMIC ORDERING GUIDE

Where dreams can become reality!

Stephen Richards

COSMIC ORDERING GUIDE

Where dreams can become reality!

First edition
Published in Great Britain

By Mirage Publishing 2006

Text Copyright © Stephen Richards 2006

First published in paperback 2006
Second print 2006

A CIP catalogue record for this book
Is available from the British Library.

ISBN 1 90257 824 4

Mirage Publishing
PO Box 161
Gateshead
NE8 4WW
Great Britain

Printed and bound in Great Britain by

Proprint
Riverside Cottages, Old Great North Road, Stibbington, Cambs, PE6 8LR

Cover designed by Sharon Anderson, Artistic Director
Cover ©Mirage Publishing

Papers used in the production of this book are recycled,
thus reducing environmental depletion.

For my friend, the mighty Cosmos

Contents

Introduction

The New Age phenomenon that has been given the name "Cosmic Ordering" has been around for years, but in a slightly different guise. For instance what does Stonehenge conjure up in the mind? It is not much different from a wishing well, or what is sometimes called a spitting stone – a stone that you spit on and make a wish. Uri Geller, the famous spoon-bender, has often appeared in newspapers and on TV, urging us to concentrate our thoughts on specific things in order to make something happen. That is Cosmic Ordering on a grand scale.

Perhaps the reason that Cosmic Ordering has not been taken seriously is that it just seems too far-fetched. Perhaps it brings to mind images of Merlin the magician, or concepts like alchemy – the notion that gold could be made with nothing more than a pestle and mortar, by grinding a few benign ingredients together. Indeed, perhaps the alchemy analogy is appropriate. With Cosmic Ordering you have the opportunity to use a metaphorical pestle and mortar to produce your own kind of gold, whether it be good health, wealth, happiness, fulfilling relationships, better status in life or increased confidence.

I have been using what is now termed Cosmic Ordering for quite a few years. At first I was like a child learning to walk. Success would come, in varying degrees, and then I would stumble and fall, demanding too much without knowing how to make it work. I didn't talk about it much because I wasn't sure of the reception I would be given if I did. But now that the UK TV presenter Noel Edmonds has given his celebrity endorsement of Cosmic Ordering, I feel I am able to walk with my head held high and give others the benefit of my guidance.

I mean, this isn't exactly something that I wanted on my résumé, as it could have branded me as an eccentric. I used to watch out for famous people using such methods, but there was no one brave enough to stick their necks out, possibly from fear of ridicule. I have my own suspicions about which celebrities use Cosmic Ordering, but Noel Edmonds has been the only one, up to now, who has been brave enough to come forward. Now that all is out in the open, I am prepared to add my name to the list of people endorsing Cosmic Ordering.

It is not a religion; but I believe that it could fast replace many of the smaller, less well-known religions with wavering followings. Noel Edmonds's introduction to the belief came when he was handed a book by a reflexologist. My own introduction was slightly different.

What I now know as the Cosmic Ordering Service was initially as alien to me as speaking Martian. The basic idea is that all things in the universe are intertwined; all reality, physics and metaphysics are one. We've all heard it said in the intro to the original *Star Trek* TV series ... words to the effect of 'time, space,' etc. Maybe Captain Kirk of the *S.S. Enterprise* was ahead of his time.

The thought of utilising energy for my own good has always fascinated me. Look how often we hear stories of how 'faith' healers use their energising hands to detect and heal illness – it is cosmic surgery. They, the healers, are using the energy of motion to create a healing technique believed to be as old as the hills. Once it was scoffed at as nothing more than quackery, but all that has changed.

The energy of life is all around us, we cannot deny this. Believers of any religion must believe in the unseen. They must open their minds to the possibility that just because something is not physically there in front of them, does not mean it does not exist. Whereas the scientist wants tangible proof that something exists, the religious person has more of an open mind.

In order to survive, we need food, water and air. But our physical bodies are not the only parts of us that we have to feed. In order to continue living, we have to nurture our spiritual beings. The cosmic believer needs the energy of the universe to survive spiritually. In this book I will show you how to obtain that energising force to nourish your feelings and expand your thoughts. Soon you will learn, and then you can make your dreams become reality.

Yes, I know there is always going to be that sceptical person hovering around, claiming: 'There's no way this is going to work.' That's fine. That was me not too long ago. I am not here to persuade anyone. All that I can do is show you what can be done. I will reveal the power of the cosmos and ask you to let it work for you, for your betterment.

We are talking about raw energy that has to be sculpted into something tangible, to be moulded into what you seek to obtain. Our actions in doing this will determine our eventual reward. Just as negativity can create an invisible force field that stops you from moving forward, Cosmic Ordering can break down barriers and get you going again.

By informing the cosmos of what we want, and by energising our requests, our desires will become reality, as if by magic. We all know that magicians use sleight of hand to deceive us into thinking that they have magically plucked a dove from thin air, when in reality they had it hidden about their person the whole time. Well, this is much the same as Cosmic Ordering. The object was there all the time, but now you are going to make it appear in front of you, in due course.

This can be done with very little conscious effort. You just need to draw on the field of energy around you, and then plug into the mass of energy that is out there in the universe. Of course, the quality of the energy has to be good, and it is no good requesting that bad things happen. The bad thing might happen as you wished, but your energy will be compromised in doing so.

Just as a car needs some sort of energy to start it up and set it in motion, so you will go about your Cosmic Ordering. You will become the mover, the catalyst, who will start a chemical reaction. I doubt any scientist would be able to prove that this is impossible. I doubt it because they already have irrefutable proof of the emission of energy from you; that is how they measure brain waves.

Our souls sparkle brightly with creative energy, our beings are as complex as the universe, and at the same time we help make up a higher body of energy. We die, but we do not cease to exist. That, however, is another matter for the sceptics to debate. Energy is still emitted from us after we die; this has been proven by scientists. With that in mind, what is wrong with the living using this energy to obtain what they desire?

The United Field Theory (UFT) is something I have subscribed to for many years; it is the theory behind Cosmic Ordering. The long dead scientist Albert Einstein had a dream of uniting electromagnetism, gravity and space. They all come together in UFT, where everything is joined as one. Well this is the same with Cosmic Ordering. You tap in to this oneness and become part of the universe as a whole. There is one difference between Einstein and me – I have successfully tapped in to the united field, he failed. Later on, I will attempt to prove the theory of UFT to you.

In order for some people to consider using the Cosmic Ordering technique, first they would want to see how nature works. But if you want to see results, then you do not need to bother yourself too much with the theory side of things. I will prove beyond doubt that it has worked for me. I will give you the documentary evidence. I want to share my experiences with you and show you that it can be done.

Just as it has worked for me, I know it can work for you in helping you to achieve your goals. When you read of how this connection with the universe has changed my life, you will, I hope, want to make similar changes to better your own life. I will also reveal many other techniques that will take you to the advanced level of Cosmic Ordering - Accelerated Cosmic Ordering.

Some people say the phenomenon of the Bermuda Triangle does not exist. Yet it cannot be denied that many vessels have disappeared inexplicably in that region. And if those same people knew that they were on a boat or ship in the midst of that mystical and deadly triangle, would they be happy to be onboard? Just as that triangle cannot be visibly seen, the same is so of the hidden universe, but it does exist.

You will be able to tap into that hidden goldmine of rewards, and I wish by the power of the cosmos that you get all that you desire. Follow my guidance and you'll find you can achieve almost anything. You can have what you want today; why wait for tomorrow?

1

The All-Seeing Cosmos

Thank you for journeying this far; it means you already have some positive thoughts and are well on the way to improving your station in life. I hope that by the time you have finished reading this guide you will have begun to believe in Cosmic Ordering, which has been so beneficial to me in my life. Firstly, though, I want to show you how any negative thoughts you might have can stunt your spiritual growth.

Let me show you how my own negativity held me back, how my pessimistic thoughts were harmful to my life. This is a true account, in a nutshell, of how my life was messed up beyond comprehension.

Have you ever watched school children playing team sports? You can usually pick out the child who has a gift for the game, who has the most skill and confidence. Equally so, you can easily tell a child who looks uncomfortable and out of place; who stands there hoping that he or she will not be called upon to act, so that they will not embarrass themselves. Well I was one of the latter.

I am not being untruthful when I tell you that I could not read or write until I was 11 years old. I had been shifted about from pillar to post so much – though I hasten to add that it was through no fault of my mother's.

I just didn't know what a stable family life was. I was from a broken home, and had seen my family torn apart by domestic violence. Already the seed of negativity was sown.

At 11 I still couldn't tie my own shoelaces, and didn't know how to tell time, or even to verbally list, with any accuracy, the chronological order of the months of the year. I wet the bed every single night until I was in my early teens, and I was bullied nearly every day of my educational life until I went to secondary school.

At one point in infant school I ended up fighting 300 of my fellow pupils at once, and I never cried. I was bloodied all over. I even caught sight of a teacher inside the school, peering out of a window and watching me. This sad excuse for a teacher made me fight with more vigour, and I actually started winning against the 300 of them. Then the bell rang for the end of what they called 'playtime'. The bullying horde went into the building as if they had done nothing wrong, or even unusual.

Why I was bullied had nothing to do with my personality. The fact of it was, I stank of urine, wore glasses, and my mother was a foreigner. The children would chant in unison at me, 'Nazi! Nazi! Nazi! Uh, uhh, uhhh. Nazi! Nazi! Nazi! Uh, uhh, uhhh!' So don't talk to me about racial abuse of the minorities – I learned all about it at a very young age. My father had been in the British Army, found himself a nice *fräulein* and brought her back to England.

So it is probably of no surprise to you when I say that every time we had a games lesson at school, I would be the last one to be picked for inclusion in team sports. Invariably, no one wanted me on their team because I was a stinking Nazi.

Years later I realised that it was, obviously, the parents and grandparents of my fellow pupils who were responsible for perpetrating these cruel acts against me by virtue of teaching their children these cruel beliefs. I had the stigma of being branded a Nazi without even knowing what a Nazi was. Of course I was not, and never have been. Nowadays the whole school would be arrested for racism, but things were not like that when I was a boy. Back then, there were no TV adverts aimed at combating bullying.

Throughout all of this I never once told my mother what I was going through, and neither did I complain to the school. Back then there was no such thing as Human Rights. But there is at least one positive aspect to all that I was put through. I believe that what I endured has helped form my strong stance against bullies.

Just out of interest, I am told that during WW II my German grandmother refused to give the *Zieg Heil* Nazi salute to an SS officer as she was coming out of a shop and he going in. It was not that she had forgotten, she just refused to conform to ideals she did not believe in. The SS officer took his handgun from his holster, held it to her head, and threatened to shoot her if she did not return his salute. The salute to the SS officer was never returned and my grandmother lived to tell the tale. I believe that, like her, most Germans hated the Nazis.

Moving on to when I was older, everything I turned my hand to went wrong. As a young man I was often quite poor. I remember a time when I was down to my last few coins, and didn't even have enough to buy a can of food for my dog. I borrowed some loose change, and while the dog ate, I went without. My love life wasn't any better. My relationship at the time had fallen into a tangled mess, and my partner left me and went back to live with her mother.

They say money can't buy you love, but obviously that was said by a wealthy loser. I can tell you this much, my empty pockets never brought me any happiness. I cursed at my life.

Even my 20-year-old car, my only prized possession, was falling apart. The morning after my partner left me I came out and tried to start it. The battery was on its last legs and didn't quite have the power to turn the engine over. My only option was to try to get the car going manually, so to speak. As I pulled hard on the steering wheel and braced my back against the central doorpost, I pushed the car backwards from its awkward parking place.

I had the driver's door fully open, and was just about to jump into the car to put it into reverse gear when there was an almighty crash! I had double-checked the road for traffic, so I knew that there wasn't anything behind the car. Confused, I turned my head and looked forward … and spotted the crumpled mess! The driver's door had caught on a lamppost and been twisted right forward to the front of the car, where it now rested against the driver's front wing. My door would now open 180 degrees, instead of 90. I had just known that something like that would happen. Maybe I even made it happen. I cursed my chaotic life.

The bitter icing on my woeful cake of life came when I was fired from my job because of staff cutbacks. I was last in and, therefore, first out. I wasn't earning much money, just enough to keep the wolves from the door, and I certainly didn't have any savings to speak of. Needless to say, this was a blow to my finances.

So there I was, living on welfare handouts, no money in my pocket or my bank, and my car damaged with little chance of being repaired. What else could go wrong? I was to find out soon enough.

Unbeknownst to me, my partner had been having an affair with a so-called drinking buddy of mine. Not only that, but at the time that she was engaging in carnal pleasure with him, she was pregnant with my child! All this came to light only after she had left me. I wasn't even aware that she was pregnant until a third party informed me. By working the dates out I knew the baby was mine.

Never mind, at least I had one friend I could still count on. I had known him since we were kids in infant school. Regardless of the bullying the others subjected me to, he had never joined the mob against me. At least I could rely on him to console me.

Back then I didn't even possess a phone, and it was quite normal for friends to knock on the door of my dark and dingy apartment unannounced. So when it happened that particular day, I was not surprised.

Just when I thought things could not get any worse, they did. My friend, my best buddy since my schooldays, had gone to a forest, and, in a depressed state, hanged himself. I was asked if I would go and identify my friend's body because his parents were devastated by his death.

I jumped into my wreck of a car, tied the door shut with an old bootlace, as I didn't even have any string, and set off. Luckily there was enough fuel in the car to take me the 25 miles to the small countryside morgue, where my friend's body was being held. To say that I was filled with dread and foreboding on the way there would be an understatement.

The deep furrow in his neck was purple-coloured and he was a ghastly sight, as they had not yet attended to him due to the involvement of the police. I had lost a very good friend, and of all the misfortunes that had befallen me of late, I mourned his loss more than anything. My head was in bits. Again, I cursed at my life.

At that point I thought that surely my life could get no worse. But I soon found out that things can always get worse when my forever-faithful dog of 8 years died from cancer. I felt useless. I was on my own, with no one around to even hear me cursing the state of it all.

I applied for job after job, knowing every time that I would not get it. I knew that every relationship I entered into would become a mess before it even happened. I knew that every car I drove would break down, be damaged in some way, or develop a fault.

I had fallen so behind with the rent on my apartment that I was served with a notice to quit. My electricity supply had been disconnected, as I could not afford the payments. I had become a sad loser and a loner. I cursed my plight to unhearing ears and unseen faces.

I had, somehow, managed to become involved in another relationship. We had not been together long when the woman I was with said she had to go into hospital for a minor procedure, and asked me if I would look after her two children while she was in. When I went to visit her in hospital it became apparent to me that she'd had an abortion. I had not even known she was pregnant.

We soon split up after that, and I always wondered why she didn't want my child. I suppose the opposite sex can spot a loser a mile off. Looking back on it, it was most likely that she had an abortion because she didn't see me as the hunter-gatherer type to provide for her and the children. Again I cursed at my wretched life.

I still mourned the death of my friend. No one could replace him, but I had to get on with my life and try to put that behind me. I built up a friendship with a biker, Lenny, who I sort of looked up to as an older brother. We became friends when I decided motorbikes were cheaper and less hassle than cars. Lenny lived with his partner, Alma, and her two children, a boy and a girl, from another relationship.

Just as the pain of my friend's death was beginning to ease, Lenny was arrested on suspicion of sexually molesting Alma's 9-year-old daughter. I attended Lenny's court hearing and heard details of the sexual assaults that had taken place over a period of several years, details that are too harrowing to write about.

The court imposed a ten-year prison sentence on Lenny, and as he was led away to the cells he couldn't even bring himself to look at anyone. My heart ached at knowing what that little girl had gone through, and is probably still going through to this very day. To say I was shocked at what Lenny had done is an understatement, as he was the least likely person you would expect to be accused of such atrocities.

The person I describe above is a world away from the person I am today. I mean, I live in a house valued at £500,000. If it were located in London it would be worth about six times this figure. I drive a luxury car, and it is not on finance – I own it outright. I have turned my life, and myself, around. From being a negative-minded loser, I have become a positive-minded winner. How did I do it?

When I began trying to make things happen in my life I grasped at any straw. I even went to some of those pyramid selling meetings you hear about, where everyone comes away with a blank stare as they think of the riches that are within their grasp. All that I would come away with was a strong thirst and a headache.

I was looking to control my own destiny, but something was missing from my life. What was that elusive magical ingredient? I would scan old newspapers lying around in betting shops and go straight to the 'opportunities' pages, where I would daydream of running my own company, being in charge of my own life.

In between races I would read of how people became rich beyond their wildest dreams whilst running a plumbing call-out service or an employment agency. All I wanted at the time was for my riches to come in on the back of the favourite I had put my money on. Invariably, I would leave the betting shop poorer than I had gone in. Again, I cursed at my wretched life and my continuous losing streak.

You see, I was mixing with losers, and so I had become a loser. You don't have to be a negative-minded person to be a loser. The betting shop was full of positive-minded people – they were all certain that the next bet they made would be the one to solve all their financial problems. They didn't see that you have to take control of your own life if you want to solve your problems, you can't simply rely on a horse. Looking back, I realize that then I had reached rock bottom. The good thing was that there was only way to go – up!

2

The Cosmic Revelation

In a desperate attempt to find solace I turned to Christianity. I would read the Bible and pray, asking God why so many horrible things had happened to me. I got no answers, nor had I expected any. When I spoke to some Christians they certainly seemed to have all the answers, but after a while I realised that all they had was the gift of the gab. At the end of the day, it was all just talk. I mean, I didn't want to have to wait for life after death for salvation. I wanted to have salvation whilst I was alive.

Don't get me wrong, I wanted it to happen and gave it all I could. I waited and waited, but no sudden changes within me took place. I did not begin speaking in tongues, or have any revelations of faith or moments of epiphany. Most of the Christians whom I met were prepared to accept whatever hand life dealt them. They would say, 'Trust in God,' and 'God will provide.' Well he had never provided for me.

It would have been easy for me to put down the beliefs of the religious, but I genuinely wanted to feel as good as they said they felt. I even took to doing some voluntary work with a Christian group, but I never felt fulfilled. One day I even knocked on the door of a vicarage for help. I explained my position, but of course the vicar could do nothing for me. I walked away cursing God's name. I soon realised that there was going to be a long wait for divine intervention from this particular source.

I could go on and tell you all about the other religions I considered, and the other methods I used in an attempt to better my life, but I am guessing that most others reading this book have been down those paths too. I do not know why or what caused the next thing to come about, but I look back on it now as some sort of divine intervention from the cosmos. At times I would catch myself thinking of my dear departed friend, often at the weirdest of times, and for no particular reason. It never occurred to me to question these thoughts, I just assumed that the memory of him would always haunt me.

With my back to the wall, I was all for throwing in the towel when, through a bizarre set of circumstances, I met a modestly wealthy man. He was Iranian, and I used to change the engine oil in his car. He didn't speak very good English at the time, and so he mistook me for a mechanic. Please don't ask why.

So there I was, every so often I would change his car's engine oil and put a new oil filter on. We became firm friends and his English rapidly improved. Initially I didn't know of his wealth, but he was a world apart from anyone else I had ever known. Nothing seemed to faze him. His philosophy was completely alien to me, but I took to it like a duck to water.

Little by little, this new friend I had discovered by accident revealed more and more of the secrets of his success. I do not mean that in a material sense, like how to make a million pounds, or how to turn poverty into riches. I mean it in a more spiritual sense – the secrets of how he was always happy and successful.

I remember the first time he invited me to an Iranian celebration. It was the Persian New Year, which is at a different time of year than the New Year of the Christian calendar. All the men were jumping over flames as a way of asking for blessings. This was my introduction to another culture at work, and it opened my eyes. They were unashamed and grateful for what they had, and were there to thank the universe for it.

Suddenly my life had started to turn itself around, and I was more than ready for change. Karl Marx once said something like 'There is no change without conflict.' Up until that point I had been blind to what life was all about. It was only then that I started to understand what it meant to be at one with one's self.

I looked back on myself and saw nothing but negativity. There was no one whom I could hold accountable for my failings in life but me. In time I learned all about being one with the cosmos, and how to make it work for me. And if that was conflict, bring it on!

I credit all of the success I now have to my conscious efforts at becoming one with the cosmos, which some claim is impossible. But it took time and energy. At first I would demand heaps of cash and other worldly goods. This was a misconception I was under. I would have had to work miracles just to manifest the amount of money in the timescale in which I had requested it.

Eventually, when I got a bit cleverer, I learned to make small, mundane demands of the cosmos. For instance, I would ask for my car not to give me any trouble, and for it to be a reliable chariot for all within it.

Shortly after making this request, I found someone wanting to swap their far better car for my old banger, reason being that they hated the colour of their car. Theirs was red, mine was a sickly green colour.

It was then that I began a habit that I still have to this day of praising my car as I drove along. I would run my hand over the dash, and the steering wheel, thanking it for how loyal it was to me. Of course, this was only when out of earshot of anyone, and while I was moving. I knew people were aware of Prince Charles speaking to his plants, but I was keen to keep the lid on my conversations with my car ... up until now.

My newfound Iranian friend had a continuous flow of wealth, so much so that he just kept giving money to his family for whatever they needed. He would give cars away, pay for holidays, and even pay for some of his family to come to England for private surgery. Because of his generosity, he didn't live as luxuriously as he could've done, but he was more than happy with what he had. It seemed that his wealth was never ending, as if he had a magic, ever-filling wallet!

Through his example, I learned a very valuable lesson. For whatever you take out of the universe, make sure you put something back, or you might run in to trouble. Remember this.

I mean, he didn't come right out and tell me he was at one with the universe, but five minutes in this man's company and it was clear that he was on a higher plane. After knowing him for some time he started to open up, especially when I introduced him to the coarse, and often vulgar, English sense of humour.

He explained to me his fear of the West, and that people would think him a bit mad for his ways and beliefs. I always had great respect for his personal beliefs, and did everything I could to show this to him. In return, I was told a series of stories that hinted at a picture that was far rosier than I had ever imagined. I was positively drooling for it to be mine.

Little by little, after many failures, I began to make things happen for me. All I had to do was follow a set of rules, and have the will to believe in what I wanted. I had to change my negative outlook and believe that what I wanted was obtainable. Initially, I may have been a little coarse in my methods, but I set my mind to learn more about what was happening to me, more about the theory and process of what is now called Cosmic Ordering.

Before long I owned a successful business. I bought into it as a partner, with no guarantee of success, but hoping that I would be able to bring in further business. I accomplished this, and soon had a nice supply of money coming in. I then used some of this extra money to make other things possible. I was on my way!

I was now mixing with positive-minded people, who would talk of foreign holidays and of test-driving this and that new luxury car. I was renting business premises from a millionaire; he talked in the language of hundreds and thousands. Soon I was as positive in my outlook as these successful people, except that I didn't have the millions. However, I was armed with an accelerant.

I previously used to put the odd bet on a horse, but even a lame donkey would beat my horse. It had been some time since I had graced a betting office with my presence, but now things were different! *Hasta la vista*, baby! Over just a few short months I won over £25,000 on the horses. My largest single win was about £5,000. Before you think that I am trying to hoodwink you, rest assured that I will prove all of these assertions later on in this guide.

I let my mind go, and though some thought my choices crazy, I always knew that I would win. I used the set of rules to call out to the cosmos, and was answered with big payouts. I did not use those so-called 'winning betting' formulae that so often fail people, I used cosmic power. I suppose I could have continued, but there is a limit to the generosity of the cosmos. After all, there would be millions of other gamblers praying to win, and someone else might get lucky. I got out while I was ahead, and after I had thanked the cosmos, I promised that I would not gamble on horses in such a way again. Besides, the bookmakers were becoming wary of my big bets and would not give me the big odds anymore. Having deprived them of their money, I moved on. I had more wishes to make come true. Armed with my winnings, courtesy of Ladbrokes, I put my money into an even more prosperous business venture.

3

Ask and the Cosmos Shall Provide

I know I have coined a phrase from Christianity for the title of this chapter, but I was sick of asking. Christianity let me down, but I now know that what I ask the cosmos for will be provided.

The two businesses I was involved in became prosperous, and I decided to open a third, larger business. I had already made my wish to the cosmos for this to happen, so I was certain that I had only to wait for the changes. As I expected, this new business was soon flourishing, and I was awash in success. I now concentrated solely on this new venture.

I didn't want to appear greedy, but I thirsted for knowledge and fulfilment. Again I followed the rules and asked the cosmos for knowledge of the mind. Soon after this I qualified as a clinical hypnotherapist. It was mind-gruelling work, but I dug deep and asked for cosmic energy to help me complete what at first seemed to be an impossible task.

Because of the domestic violence I had been forced to endure as a child, I wanted to help others. I had witnessed some of the worst scenes a child could ever imagine, so I understood what emotional pain was all about. Most of these are too grisly to recount in a book, but there are a few that I will tell you about.

After being shifted from pillar to post, my mother secured a live-in housekeeping job for a man called Danny. Danny initiated a relationship with my mother, and it wasn't long before they became embroiled in a quagmire of domestic arguments. More often than not, my mother would walk out on Danny, taking me with her. We would go and stay with a nearby female friend my mother had.

At the time, I had a white pet rabbit, who I had named Snowy. After another domestic row, my mother and I walked out. When we returned to Danny's house, I ran straight to where I used to keep my pet rabbit. I found Snowy lying dead, still and stiff. I was only four, but I had already become hardened by witnessing gross acts of domestic violence. I had even seen a dead woman lying in an open-lidded coffin, in someone else's home. So I didn't cry at the sight of Snowy, with blood on his lips and nose. I just held him close to me, smelling his fluffy fur.

The pain of such a tragedy simply sunk in, to be locked away in another sacred box, and put alongside all the others I had stored in my heart. Later, I found out that Snowy had been smashed to death against a wall. He had been held by his rear legs and smashed to oblivion before his lifeless body was slung into a corner of the cupboard where I kept him. The killer was Danny.

Before we moved in with Danny, my mother and I lived with another man, her husband, Hughie (not my father). I believe this marriage came about when my father deserted my mother, leaving her in limbo. I recall nothing but violence while my mother was with Hughie. I remember an incident where he held a handgun to my mother's head, telling her to make his tea. He then threw a dish of water over her head. Every time I saw Hughie's shadow pass the window of the small riverside cottage as he was returning home, I would scream the place down.

One day my mother decided to leave Hughie, so she took me by the hand and we went out of the house. I remember the two of us sitting forlornly in an open cornfield, until somehow Hughie came across us. He had probably been tipped off by the policeman who had questioned my mother shortly before. He had asked here where we lived. 'Here, in the field,' she replied.

I was only three at the time, but I can still see the tall, dark, brooding figure of Hughie as he dragged my mother home through the fields by her hair, backwards along the ground. I remember screaming in terror at the thought of what he would do to her.

Eventually, when my mother could bear it no longer, she left Hughie for good. Initially we lived in a disused hut. My mother used a hacksaw blade to saw the hooks off the ceiling. She claimed she was trying to make the place more presentable, but she probably feared that if Hughie found us he would hang her from one of the hooks. That is how much fear this man evoked in my mother. I could tell you far more, but I have no desire to launder private family laundry in public and, hey, you are here for your requests to be granted by the cosmos.

Largely because of these early experiences, I had an overwhelming desire to help people through emotional trauma. Undoubtedly this prompted my thirst for knowledge. I eventually qualified as a stress counsellor, and then branched out to other divisions of counselling, qualifying in a number of disciplines. I continued my higher education and won many more professional qualifications, all thanks to the mighty cosmos. My request for knowledge had been granted.

I was working as a therapist on the side, and soon I was curing people who had all sorts of hang-ups and problems: emotional traumas, sexual dysfunctions, phobias, past lives and the like. I pride myself on having cured an agoraphobic, who had suffered for some 16 years, in a single one-hour session using an open-eyed clinical hypnotherapy technique. I no longer work in clinical hypnosis, as the number of people I have helped has more than fulfilled me, but I still get the odd request for help from those close to me, which I freely give. I was, when administering curative hypnotherapy, simply a medium of cosmic healing.

My thirst for cosmic knowledge continued, and I studied as much as I could. I sought out anything to do with the cosmos (universe). Back then, though, I was chasing what is called the United Field Theory (UFT), not Cosmic Ordering.

Within each of us lies a dormant power waiting to be unleashed; it just takes some know-how and regular use of the rules to unlock this hidden potential. This phenomenon is not just about listing your demands – you cannot demand things from the cosmos. But with learning and understanding you can make things happen yourself.

What I am going to tell you now may sound familiar, but I asked for a bigger challenge in life. Although my cash and carry business was still up and running, it didn't take an Einstein to operate it. I know the UK TV presenter Noel Edmonds made a similar request of the cosmos ... and he got it, too!

As a sideline I had been authoring booklets, and I was selling these via advertisements in opportunity magazines. Most of the 60 or so titles I authored were not very memorable and never won me any prizes: *Forever Young* (how to stay young looking), *How to Win on the Lottery* (from which I had a small amount of success with the system I devised), etc, etc. But I had a hankering to do more than just sell these poorly put together booklets.

Having cut my teeth in the publishing business with my booklets, it was a natural progression to become one of those big shot publishers I was always reading about. I could have asked to become a Hollywood movie star, but somehow I didn't think the Cosmic Ordering Service stretched to miracles of that magnitude.

So in 1998 I opted for the alternative to becoming a movie star by starting up a new publishing company. That was certainly a challenge. Soon I was classed as a 'maverick' of the publishing world. Though it wasn't exactly praise, I even became excited when the *Times* described my company as 'an obscure publisher'. Well, I did ask the cosmos for publicity, but forgot to add the word 'positive'.

Before long I sold the cash and carry business to concentrate on publishing, and went on to publish quite a few books. Soon things were coming my way faster than I could ever have expected, and with little effort on my part. My first major breakthrough came with the rock star Sting's authorised biography.

The authorised biography of Sting was serialised in one of the UK's biggest selling Sunday newspapers, the *News of the World*. The book was written by Sting's best friend, so it wasn't even something that I had had to write. Of course, Sting supported it and gave a multitude of media interviews to help sales.

Soon I was publishing more books by other authors, and co-authoring and ghost-writing books for other people. More serialisations of books I authored appeared in UK national newspapers, and I was being given money for something I loved doing.

I even starred in TV documentaries and have since helped some 100 or so TV companies throughout the world with documentaries relating to true crime. During all of this, not once was I brave enough to mention my friend the cosmos. Who would have believed me back then anyway?

My success spiralled to new heights when I was on this and that radio show throughout the UK, even appearing on the news channels and Teletext. I have worked with so many stars that I have lost count. In particular, though, I have worked with the actor Ray Winstone when he gave his help towards a fund-raising book my company published. A whole host of celebrities also helped: Sir Elton John, Cilla Black, Lulu, Ruby Wax, Elizabeth Hurley, Michael Winner, Roger Daltrey, Richard Branson, Sir Trevor McDonald, Billy Murray, Jimmy White, Stephen Hendry, Chris Tarrant and numerous others.

I had gotten more than I hoped for when, in the course of my everyday job, I got to meet all sorts of celebrities, from the actor Sir Ben Kingsley to the boxer Ernie Shavers. I even had the actress Samantha Janus helping to promote a book for me, so I think, perhaps, the cosmos has had just a little hand in helping me become a big shot.

Having asked the cosmos to use my status as a writer to inspire others, I was rewarded when people started sending me letters telling me how I was doing just that. I even received a congratulatory letter from Sir John Stephens, the then Commissioner of the Metropolitan Police Force. Even the famous Jeremy Beadle was advising me about my writing style. We spoke on the phone numerous times; he's an unselfish and giving man. You can forget the old TV persona of Jeremy Beadle; the man is a true diamond.

I wanted to make my writing different, I wanted it to help people … and again, the cosmos helped me. I am pleased to say that I was able to work with victims of some of the highest profile paedophiles in the UK: Fred and Rose West, and Ian Huntley. My writing helped sexual abuse victims come to terms with what had happened to them. Even now, I am still working on books aimed at victims of sexual abuse. I thank the cosmos for allowing me to be of help to others.

Having met the challenge of being a successful publisher, I still own the Mirage Publishing imprint. I now also write for a top London publisher. I have started up another business interest that is fast becoming more lucrative than I had ever thought possible, catapulting me into the realms of millionaire status! I believe what I have already gained is not half nor quarter of what I will gain, and all because of Cosmic Ordering.

I have so many other stories to tell, and ways to help you develop your own cosmic skills, but that is for later on when I will reveal an abundance of ways in which you can make the cosmos work for you. Some claim that Cosmic Ordering is 'piffle' and that it is 'because you are "lucky" that you will get what you want.' To this I say, 'Piffle.' Look at my earlier life; was I lucky to get all of that trouble? I could fill this book twice over with the traumatic experiences I had.

Here are just a few examples of what I endured as a child, and it is not one hundredth of the ill that happened to me prior to Cosmic Ordering changing my life. I had three puppies in succession, which, one after the other, were run over and killed by a baker's van. In the end I was refused another puppy from the litter, as they had all been gifts.

I nearly died from swallowing a pickled onion that got stuck in my throat when I was five years old. I was saved by a man who threw me over his knee and whacked me on my back. The onion popped out and I could breathe again.

When I was six years old, I was lifted off the ground and strangled by a lodger at a boarding house my mother and I were staying in. I believe this deranged man would have murdered me if someone had not come across us in time.

When I was seven years old, I jumped from the roof of a shed, and somehow got tangled in a washing line. I swung by my neck, choking. I survived by the narrowest of margins.

I spent six weeks in a children's home when I was nine years old. This was not through any fault of my mother; she had to have surgery and no one would look after me. I spent that time wondering what was going on, before eventually being reunited with her.

The account I have given of my life is a much-watered down version, but I just wanted to convey the type of life I have led. I certainly was not born with a silver spoon in my mouth. Back then, we were lucky to have spoons made of tin.

We were so poor that we could not even afford a toothbrush, never mind the toothpaste. I remember having to rub my finger in the soot in the back of the fireplace, and using my sooted finger to clean my teeth. Sometimes my mother would boil and mash some old, woody turnips, and I would invite my poor friends around for a feast, or so it seemed. That, to us, was a luxury. Nowadays, I guess, kids would turn their noses up at such a meal.

In the winter, when it became unbearably cold, we had to use coats and towels as makeshift blankets. All that kept us warm in the day was a coal fire, and since we could not afford the coal, we used anything else that would burn, so long as it cost nothing.

I was not a naturally gifted or lucky person; it seemed everything was against me. I tried a lot of things to help me overcome my poverty, and so far only Cosmic Ordering has worked. So I thank the cosmos for making it all happen.

4

Cosmic Gods

I wonder, have you ever heard of a man called Erich von Däniken? Well, for those of you not familiar with his work I can tell you that he is the most successful non-fiction writer of all time. I want to qualify how seriously people take him, and that way I can add some depth to what I will reveal hereon in.

It would be easy for me to write a book giving you a brief outline of what Cosmic Ordering is all about, but I guess it might leave some of you feeling short-changed. My aim is to make it abundantly clear to you that we all have the inert skills to communicate our desires to the cosmos. The secret to Cosmic Ordering, though, is having those desires manifest before you. I do, however, make this proviso; you must believe that it will happen. Your dreams will come true, but do not be overly demanding. Be logical – there are not enough mansions for everyone in the world, are there? At least not yet. Be prepared to get it little by little, if that is what it takes.

I first read books by Erich von Däniken when I started to become more selective in my reading choices. What struck me was the man's belief in what he wrote; he never wavered. Whether I believed what I read within his books is another matter. However, I did learn something from this man who has sold over 60 million copies of his books worldwide.

For over 40 years, Erich von Däniken has pursued the theory that Earth might have been visited by extraterrestrials in the remote past. What I am getting at here is the belief his readers have in what he does. They might never have met the man, and may never have seen any proof of aliens (unless they believe what they see on *Star Trek*), but they mostly all choose to believe him.

Well, that is the unwavering belief you must learn to develop in Cosmic Ordering. You must believe, without seeing, that your order is on its way. Never waver from that belief.

Let me tell you a story that illustrates the sort of belief you must have in yourself. Two rival footwear companies want to expand their European sales operations into Africa. Each employs a top salesman and gives them the overblown job title of 'Senior Sales Director of the African Sector'.

After a week, one of the salesmen makes a telephone call to the European HQ of his company and says, 'You are not going to believe this, no one over here wears shoes. It is going to be a waste of time. I'm coming home.'

The rival salesman also calls his HQ and tells them, 'Wow, you are not going to believe this! No one here is wearing any shoes, send me as many pairs as you can.'

These two differing attitudes to the same situation equally apply to you. If you only see the negative points, then how are you going to be able to sit down and work out how to achieve the things you want? You have to begin to believe in yourself, you have to do that right from this moment. Do not merely pretend that you believe in your wishes, actually sit down and visualise them. Should you even have the slightest doubt in what you are doing, and feel yourself becoming negative, then that is the time to concentrate even more on isolating, and even eradicating, those thoughts. You have to think of these negative thoughts as thieving hands, coming to get what you are wishing for.

When I say that the theory of extraterrestrial contact is not as illogical as it might first seem, there may be sceptics out there who meet that opinion with negative thoughts. But I am not aiming to please the sceptics amongst you. This is not a guide about self-improvement, but a guide for self-fulfilment. I want to reveal some of my learning, and to help form your mind in readiness for cosmic action. The debate about whether aliens walked the ancient earth thousand of years ago goes on, and gets stronger by the day.

My point is that if we have had alien influences, then perhaps we need to begin to take advantage of what lies dormant within us. It is not something I want to take to the grave with me. A most incredible claim made by von Däniken is that we are descendants of these galactic pioneers. Now if that is the case then surely we must have a dormant ability within us - some untapped brainpower.

We each have an inert sixth sense that over the passage of time has become dulled from lack of use. This stems from the days when we needed to use our intuition more than our other five senses: feeling, smelling, tasting, seeing and hearing. There are theories of parallel universes out there, which no one can prove or disprove.

But more importantly, where do such theories come from, and who lives in these universes if they exist?

Déjà vu haunts us all at some time or another – I should know given the amount of Past Lives Therapy I have administered. Things people could not have consciously known are locked deep within their minds, and under hypnosis are revealed. After these sessions, dates, places, and names from the past have all been verified. Who am I to argue with fact? I have been taught to accept people and their beliefs unconditionally, and I use that dictum in believing that the cosmos will provide.

Our sixth sense is what prompted me to look more closely at what it is that could be within us. Where does it come from, how does it work? Once we learn how to connect to our untapped resources, a new avenue of exploration is opened up.

I have watched sceptics being interviewed on TV, and they all attribute the success of Cosmic Ordering to nothing more than luck, or a twisted ego trying to win publicity. I am not prepared to stand up and argue against them. Their negative minds are closed and these people will always be emotionally stunted. Some atheists argue against there being a god, while religious believers look upon them with derision. Do not get entangled or embroiled in similar arguments over Cosmic Ordering. There is nothing to prove to anyone, just concentrate on your own needs.

When former England soccer manager/coach Glenn Hoddle said in *The Times* that people born with disabilities were paying for their past lives, he was sacked from his position, amidst controversy. This assertion was something that went far deeper than a newspaper interview could ever convey, and he suffered the backlash of his theory. If you have beliefs that are outside of the mainstream, you are often made to pay for them, or at the very least, ridiculed.

All that I will say is that it took a brave man like Noel Edmonds to come out in the open by attributing his revitalised success to Cosmic Ordering. I have only come out of the closet thanks to him. This 'coming out' by Noel Edmonds could have seriously backfired on him, as in Glenn Hoddle's case. So, in a way, I actually have the cosmos to thank for making all of this happen, via Mr Edmonds. Without him, this guide would probably not have been published. I did not fancy becoming something for people to ridicule, and I do not want to be considered to be talking mumbo-jumbo. But now that all is out in the open, I do not care how many sceptics knock Cosmic Ordering.

I have asked the cosmos for this guide to be accepted by as many people as possible as a fuller explanation of what it is all about, as opposed to a misquoted shorter piece of work. I owe it to the cosmos, by way of thanks for all of the success it has given me.

Swiftly moving away from that controversial issue, I now move on to another issue that is equally as controversial, the third eye! Did you know that the image we see with our eyes is viewed upside-down? It is only when the image is sent to the brain that it is turned the right way up. That is how technical our brains are. Although we are all (for the most part) blessed with two visible eyes, we do have another eye – a third eye that has become dormant and obsolete due to lack of use.

Scientifically known as the pineal gland, the third eye is considered to have mystical powers. Just imagine that: having a Mystical Third Eye and not even using it.

'Where is it located?' I hear you ask. For any of you who are good at geometry, which I am not, it is located in the geometric centre of the brain, right behind the pituitary gland, and it is pea sized. For a more definite location, if we could go right to the root of our nose then we would find it, attached to the third ventricle.

With the medical parlance out of the way, I can now go on to the real meaning of the third eye, its spiritual function. Well, just as Einstein tried to unify things in the United Field Theory, the third eye, the seat of the soul, controls the various biorhythms of the body. It unites them. In fact, the ancient Greeks thought the gland to be responsible for our connection to the Realms of Thought.

The gland needs one special ingredient to activate it, light. It works in perfect harmony with the hypothalamus gland, which in turn controls our bodies ageing process, our biological clock. Oh, and it controls our body's desire for thirst, hunger, and sex.

'What is all this leading to?' you might well ask. And 'Why', you may further ask, 'doesn't he get to the point?' Well, I could just tell you my basic principle of Cosmic Ordering, and let you get on with it, hoping for the best. By comparison, it would be like me throwing a non-driver the keys to a car and telling them to get on with it. Without them knowing how to put the car into gear and letting the handbrake off, they wouldn't move!

I feel responsible for preventing you from crashing your car, as you might blame me for a lack of effort in passing on my own skills. I am going to show you how to start the process of putting your mind in motion, just like with a car. First, you master the basics, and then you can go on to the next stage.

This is why I would ask you to follow my guidance. So back to the pineal gland: until recent times the physiological function of the gland had been lost to us. The old school of thought about its function was that it was the connecting link between the physical and spiritual worlds. Hopefully you are now starting to understand the reason for my taking you into the realms of physiology.

Later, when you use your pineal gland to connect to a higher frequency you may feel a pressure at the base of the brain. Similarly, a head injury can be responsible for activating the gland. This gland is considered to be the most powerful and highest source of ethereal energy available to humans, and has always been important in initiating supernatural powers. Which leads me on to my point: development of psychic talents has been attributed to this organ of higher vision.

I feel it wise to say that it is not what you can see, but rather what you cannot see that is being focused on here. The third eye can see beyond the physical as it looks out through what some people call the chakra system. This is accomplished when we contemplate (some call it meditate). As a clinical Hypnotherapist, meditation is something I have always prescribed. In fact, it is self-hypnosis.

I don't want to overly complicate things here, so let's keep it simple. When I tell you that during the course of the day you will go into trance about half a dozen times without realising it then, I hope that I am making it less sinister. I am paving the way for you to grasp what lies ahead.

The stage hypnotist has given hypnosis a bad name, even inducing fear in people. I can assure you, there is nothing to fear. When you are on the phone, you are often in a semi-trance, losing all track of reasonable time, almost thrown into a different world. This is what a hypnotic state is like, not much different from being on the phone. I can assure you, you cannot be made to do anything against your will or anything that is unsafe. I leave parlour games, such as making people run around clucking like chickens, to the likes of third-rate pub and club acts that use naturally extroverted people to show off in front of their friends.

Going off into meditation is simple. Just sit and look out of the window, relax and have some of your favourite music playing. You certainly do not need incense sticks or candles burning around the room, unless these things create an ambience that helps you feel relaxed. Taking the phone off the hook and relaxing is the basis for meditation. It's simple.

We all use meditation, often without being aware of it, when looking for answers from a higher place, a higher frequency. You might have to sit and think things through before making a major decision – that is meditation. Sometimes people say, 'Let me sleep on it'. That is also meditation.

The pineal gland plays several significant roles in human functioning and contains a complete map of the visual field of the eyes. That is all you need to know, as the medical terms are mind-boggling! Putting it simply, have you ever heard of Seasonal Affective Disorder (SAD)? This medically recognised condition is usually brought on by lack of light, often in the winter months, and people can become a little depressed and grumpy.

There is a pathway from the retinas to the hypothalamus which brings information about light and dark cycles. From there nerve impulses travel via the pineal nerve to the pineal gland. The production of melatonin is inhibited during these processes, and when there is no light stimulating the hypothalamus, usually at night, pineal inhibition ceases and melatonin is released. Which, in layman's terms, means that the light and dark cycles (night and day), affect how the pineal gland works as an important timekeeper for the human body.

It is only natural that when we sit and relax, and stare off into the distance in deep thought, that something is going on in our heads. During relaxation and visualisation (which is simply seeing yourself getting into that new car, or boarding the plane for a holiday) the pineal gland secretes melanin.

The electromagnetic energy that created us allows us to become one with that same energy that is around us, and this is done through the pineal gland. Hence the reason for me going on about it. At some point you are going to have to sit down and contemplate what I have said. I would hope that by that point, some of these subliminal meanings that I have thrown in would have soaked through your system, allowing things to happen to you for the better.

The line of communication with the higher plain is via an activated pineal gland. Without being too clever, I want to show you how this happens. What is called the 'crown chakra' reaches down until its vortex touches the pineal gland. Something that is called *Prana* (pure energy) is received through this energy centre in the head.

Do not become too concerned over this explanation, as soon it will all become second nature. You will be able to communicate with the cosmos whenever you want, and you will be able to convey your desires in a more effective manner than writing out a wish list and sticking it under your pillow or burning it. These are reinforcement methods for beginners, and although I am not knocking it, as it does work, it is a hit and miss method.

It is a little like pressing buttons at random on the telephone keypad and expecting to speak to the person you thought about calling. You might strike lucky and hit the correct buttons, but in reality I believe you would have more chance of winning the lottery: 14 million to one! Well, by comparison, the method I will show you to connect to the cosmos will be like hitting the redial key. Every time you want a connection it will be right at your mental fingertips.

Activating the pineal gland (sometimes called the 'third eye') is like putting a key into the lock of a door that opens into a warehouse full of luxuries. Getting the key into the lock happens when you reach an absolute state of meditation, where you are ready to enter a higher dimension of thought. Without going into complicated scientific language, getting the pineal and pituitary glands to vibrate in unison will make the turning of the key in the lock possible.

You do not have to have concerns as to how you are going to activate the pineal gland. There is no need for you to do anything other than enter a state of meditation or relaxation. The more relaxed and deeper in thought you become, the greater the chances of this happening.

During relaxation, if you were connected to a machine capable of detecting electromagnetic current, it would give a positive reading to show that a magnetic field is created. This allows a relationship between personality, operating through the pituitary body, and the soul, operating through the pineal gland. So all you need do is sit there, relax, and enjoy the ride.

We have often heard of people talking about the light at the end of the tunnel after they have been pulled back from death's door. Nearly all of the stories relate to a light, a sense of being drawn to it, and an out-of-body experience. Well, do not worry too much about the out-of-body experience; we just need to concentrate on turning the light at the end of the tunnel on.

How do you turn the light on? Simple: the negative and positive forces interact and become strong enough to create the light, which is inside your mind. Now this is rather like a fridge light. When we open the fridge door the light comes on, but how do we know for sure that it goes out when we close the door?

Even if we manipulate the little spring-loaded switch that is near the hinge, and by so doing can make the light go on and off, how do we know that the light is definitely out when the door is shut? So it is with the 'light in the head'. We cannot actually open our heads to see if the light is on or if it comes on, but it is quite possible that the light is on.

The only way of seeing if the light in our minds is on is to use an 'illumined awareness'. I do not want to enter into the realms of astral projection, which is a related subject, but not one I want to go into detail about in this book. However, I will say that when this light is activated, some people subscribe to the notion that astral projectors can withdraw themselves from their bodies, and carry the light with them. Should you get to that stage then I would be very interested in hearing your thoughts on the subject.

I believe astral projection to be quite different to how the layman thinks it to be. There is a part of the mind that is so powerful that it can challenge the bounds of physics. Astral travel, as well as other occult abilities, is closely associated with the development of this inner light. This is probably why the lights appear to those who have had near-death experiences. I believe the state necessary for this higher plain to be reached is probably at its closest when we are near death.

So how do we bring about a near-deathlike state without being injured, or actually dying? Well, there is a way to do this through self-hypnosis or with physical relaxation, and it is as safe as thinking of the directions given to get from A to B. Personally, I believe self-hypnosis is the best way to do this as you can take yourself into a far deeper state of relaxation, whilst still being in control. I will go into this in more detail in a later chapter.

I know you must wonder where this is taking you, as you probably thought this was going to be something far different than my going on about the third eye. But rest assured that it is relevant to what I want to show you. Imagine that I am your driving instructor. I am not going to show you how to drive a formula one (F1) car, but I will show you how to drive safely. If, later on, you want to drive an F1 racing car, then good luck. Come back and tell me when you are world champion and you can do my cosmic connecting for me.

Certainly you do not need to know how the engine works in order to be able to drive the car. This chapter was to show you the resources available within you, and how to gain access to accelerated Cosmic Ordering. I want to show you how you can fast track your requests, as I have done. Using your mind is a faster method to getting what you want. I mean, all you have to do is sit there. What could be easier?

5

Fast Track Your Cosmic Order

Think of us humans as living in a giant greenhouse. Given the greenhouse gasses that are worrying mankind now, this notion does not seem unrealistic. Outside of that greenhouse is the universe. My aim is to show you how to connect to what is outside of the greenhouse, to be able to transcend the bonds of nature, to become one with what is outside. You cannot do it physically, as it is impossible to breach the greenhouse glass. Yet you know there is something outside, and you need a means of communicating your desires to it.

Similarly, we need some way to communicate with the higher plain, to be able to reach it with our thoughts, to tap into the whole system. Yes, we can send handwritten notes via a hot air balloon, but how do we know that they get there? It is all rather hit and miss. Even if the note does get there, how will we receive what we requested in the note? Why send a letter when you can use the phone? That is what I want to show you. Yes, by all means use snail mail, but how do you know it has reached its destination? It could be lost in the post. Your wish may be granted 30 years hence. How often have you heard of letters being delivered 30 years after they were posted? It has happened. I know the success rate of mail being delivered is very high, probably near to 99 per cent, maybe more. But do you want to risk being one of the negative statistics whose mail has not gotten there at all, never mind in 30 years time? You need some means of assurance, a sort of fast track number where you can call someone up and say, 'Hey, I ordered this last week, when can I expect delivery?'

The threads that connect us to the earth also connect us to different constellations and to a system of electromagnetic fields that are responsible for life. Call the electromagnetic field 'God' if you want, as it is all around us. These are the signals scientists watch out for in the universe, signs of other life. There are googols and googols (the number 1 with 100 zeroes behind it) of these waves flying about out there. You just have to hit one, and then you have your connection.

Perhaps some of you believe I have gone into the realms of the impossible, where little green men are running around on some other planet. I am sure that when I tell you that there is a small bottle containing a red fluid on a shelf in Sheffield University's microbiology laboratory, and that the phial contains the first samples of extraterrestrial life isolated by researchers, well, it might prompt you to believe my claim.

On 25 July, 2001, blood-red rain fell over the Kerala district of western India. The rain bursts continued for two months, turning local people's clothes pink, burning leaves on trees and at some points falling as scarlet sheets. Inside the bottle mentioned above is a sample of this rain, surely one of the strangest incidents to occur in recent meteorological history. Claims were made that the rain was red because winds had swept up dust from Arabia and dumped it on Kerala.

A physicist, Godfrey Louis, at Mahatma Gandhi University in Kottayam, debunked this claim after gathering samples left over from the rains. 'If you look at these particles under a microscope, you can see they are not dust, they have a clear biological appearance,' said Louis. In short, it rained aliens over India during the summer of 2001. Although the evidence was not fully conclusive, and the claim was even ridiculed by a scientist who called it 'bullshit', a few researchers believe Louis may have been on to something and are following up on his work.

I don't want to go too fully into this, as nothing has been proven and this guide is not the place for scientific argument, but I just wanted to show you the possibility of other life forms being out there. And just as that is a possibility, there is also the possibility of you making that cosmic connection happen for you.

The 'Big Bang' theory of how the universe was made is as near to being true as ever. Something spectacular obviously happened in the universe, then something went wrong and life had to evolve in separate parts of the universe, but the cosmic connection was never fully severed. Rather like a crossed phone connection or bad mobile phone reception, we can hear the conversations of others, albeit in bits and pieces.

Touching on the red rain story again, Louis also discovered that hours before the first red rain fell, there was a loud sonic boom that shook houses in Kerala. Perhaps it was an incoming meteorite. Only such a thing could have triggered such a blast, he claims. As the meteorite shot towards the coast it could have shed microbes. Louis related this to the theory of the late Fred

Hoyle, the British theorist, who argued that life on Earth evolved from microbes brought here on comets.

Using this as an example, we might be able to accept that we are not the sole occupants of the galaxy, and that there is a higher race that we have possibly evolved from. I keep an open mind, as I would ask you to do. That being said, never having seen this higher race, how can scientists talk of such a phenomenon and not be laughed at? The science of Cosmic Ordering is far more believable to most people than the idea of little green men running around on some distant planet. Bearing that in mind, why should you be ridiculed just because you sat down for half an hour and had private thoughts about what you want out of life? Everyone does it, we all dream.

Perhaps if we had only the red rain as evidence that there might be an alien race out there then we could rid ourselves of outlandish notions like Cosmic Ordering. If there were aliens then what would be the point of us wanting to make contact with the cosmos? But when you think about it you must see how unlikely that is to work. Surely we could not rely solely on another human helping us. By that I mean that we would send some sort of signal out to the cosmos in the hope that the man in the imaginary warehouse would intercept it, and then send us our order without any demand for payment.

There has to be a higher order of intelligence for this to work. Even if the owners of the intelligence have long since ceased to exist, the electrical energy continues to exist in electromagnetic fields. What do you think happens to the signals sent out from a radio station? Where do you think they go, and do you think they just die and fizzle out after travelling through the air? How can they just die and end as nothing, how can these waves just cease to exist?

To give you an example of how things can live on long after those that have made it have ceased to exist, look at the Great Pyramid. It is the only survivor of the seven ancient wonders. Located in Cairo, Egypt, the pyramid still amazes thousands of scientists and guests each year. When you look at the magnificence of this piece of architectural wonder, built over a period of 20 years, and when you think that even with our technology, we would not be able to construct something in this day and age that would compare, how can you deny the existence, at some point, of something far superior to modern day mankind?

There are a great many theories as to how and who built the pyramids, but none of them can satisfactorily explain how it was done. How did Egyptians manage to haul stones weighing as much as 20 tons up hundreds of feet? The Great Pyramid was the biggest and tallest of all the Pyramids ever built. Since the Egyptians left us very detailed written records, you would think that the building of the greatest pyramid would be discussed. It is not.

The Pyramid was referred to a few times in very early hieroglyphics. Egyptian writing suggests the Great Pyramid was standing before Egyptians populated the land. Ancient hieroglyphics never mentioned the actual building of the pyramids.

Ancient Egyptian writings often talk of beings from the sky, of the sky opening and bright lights coming down to give them technology and wisdom. Many pictures and symbols resemble UFOs and aliens. Some higher intelligence must have existed to build the pyramids. In order for you to consider such things possible, I need you to open your mind. Consider this a mind opening exercise.

The pyramids are so accurately aligned with the points of the compass that only a higher intelligence could have achieved this all those thousands of years ago. The angle of the slope of the sides is so precise, at 52 degrees. In 2500 BC man did not have the tools or knowledge necessary to build the pyramids. Given that lifting gear and cranes were not around at that time, what other method could have been used? Can you allow your mind to open far enough for you to come to the same conclusion most other intelligent people would?

Imagine the intelligence needed to create the Sphinx, or the Great Pyramid of Giza, one of the most impressive structures on Earth. About 2,550 BC, King Khufu, the second pharaoh of the fourth dynasty, commissioned the building of his tomb at Giza. Some Egyptologists believe it took somewhere in the region of 80 years to construct the pyramid. Its weight is six million tons. The four corners are almost perfect right angles and align almost exactly to the four points of the compass.

Conventional wisdom holds that the pharaohs commissioned the building of the Pyramids as elaborate burial grounds for when they died. Alternative theory holds that the Pyramids and Sphinx were used for more practical purposes like navigation and power generation.

According to one alternative theory, Egyptians had help from an extra-terrestrial race to construct the pyramids. This would also explain why the pyramids are lined up in the formation of the stars on Orion's Belt. When superimposed, the pyramids at Giza are in the exact position as those stars. Several other astrological phenomena can be associated with the placement and position of the pyramids. Measurements of different aspects of the Great Pyramids demonstrate amazing knowledge of mathematics.

For example, if the perimeter of the pyramid is divided by twice its height the result is 3.14159. This happens to be the first six digits of pi. Pi is also the relation of many of the other measurements throughout the pyramid. Mathematical accuracy like this is thought by some to be too advanced for such an ancient civilization.

Many of the passages within the pyramid have curious calculations as well. When added up, the length of some passages equal specific dates in time, dates that were in the distant future in the time of the Egyptians. Some of the dates relate to the life and death of Christ, important happenings in the history of the Jews, and events of global proportion.

Whatever you decide, surely you would have to agree that it would take a great intelligence to perform such a feat of architecture. We cannot explain how, but the pyramids exist. Just as the impossible exists, so too does Cosmic Ordering. Just as some ancient architect was able to visualise the Great Pyramid, you too will be able to visualise what you want to achieve in life, and then see it realised.

There are great similarities with the Cydonia site on Mars, which some say is evidence that an extra-terrestrial race helped in the construction of the pyramids. Early pictures of the surface of Mars showed what looked to be a face, with pyramid-like monuments located nearby. However we look at it, whether it is a face on

Mars, or the unexplained Great Pyramid, we have to admire the sheer scale of it all, and the role we all play in the mighty universe. There is even a suggestion of the desire of ancient Egyptians to return to another planet, which could have been their original home. Who are we to argue?

I have said that the three Pyramids of Giza are exactly aligned with the three stars in the belt of Orion, both in position and in size. In fact, at the time that the pyramids were supposedly built (about 3000 BC), the stars that make up the Belt of Orion were not exactly at the correct angle to match up with the pyramids. If the position of the stars is traced back over thousands of years, the time at which the belt is exactly aligned with the pyramids would have been 10,500 BC. A time when there were supposedly no civilised humans living on the earth.

The Sphinx was actually built in 10,500 BC, around the same time as the pyramids. If you consider the Sphinx, a lion with a human head, you can see that the body is perfectly proportioned for the head of a lion, not the head of a human. The human head looks tiny and silly sitting on top of the body. This is because the Sphinx was actually built in 10,500 BC, around the same time as the pyramids, with the head of a lion. Another impossible feat.

You must wonder how the Pyramids of Giza, supposedly built in 3,000 BC, are still standing as tall and perfect as the day they were completed? The other Pyramids, which were said to have been built about 500 years later, all have shoddy masonry, and are crumbling down. An example of this is the famous 'bent' pyramid, which starts out with the sides being built at one angle, then suddenly shifts in the middle to a shallower angle. Perhaps this is merely an imitation of the real thing. They say imitation is the best form of flattery. Equally so, prayer has its roots in Cosmic Ordering.

I believe that the Egyptian pharaohs saw the great pyramids standing on their land and decided that they wanted pyramids of their own. But they found that it was much harder to do than expected, and ended up building silly-looking structures that do not even come close to the elegance of the great pyramids. Just think, Cosmic Ordering has to be given some consideration as being the prototype of ancient beliefs. Man would look to the sky and ask for rain, or ask for the rain to stop. His request was granted. In time, people wanted their own cosmic creation, an imitation of the real thing. Why should religion have the monopoly on requests of the cosmos, or prayers to God?

I remind you that if you take the perimeter of the pyramid and divide it by two times the height, you get a number that is exactly equivalent to Pi (3.14159...), up to the fifteenth digit. The chances of this happening by chance are remarkably small. Did the ancient Egyptians know the value of Pi? Bear in mind that this was a number not calculated accurately to the fourth digit until the 6th century, and the pyramids calculate it to the fifteenth digit. What cosmic power was involved in the Great Pyramid scam? That is what I believe it was, a red herring of sorts. Perhaps even something that started as a folly to keep higher beings entertained, until unworthy copies were made.

Here is another thought to ponder: if you take the lines of longitude and latitude that the pyramid lies on, 31 degrees north by 31 degrees west, you will find that they are the two lines that cover the most combined land area in the world. In essence, the pyramid is the centre of all of the landmass of the whole earth! The height of the pyramid (481 feet) is almost exactly 1/1,000,000,000 of the distance from the earth to the sun (480.6 billion feet)!

Now that the history and architecture lessons are over, what about Pyramid Power, where does it come into the equation of Cosmic Ordering? Well, this is where I was leading you. I could have gone straight in to Pyramid Power, but I felt my little digression might make it more of an adventure for you.

The phrase 'pyramid power' was coined back in 1973, attributed to Patrick Flanagan. He used these words to describe the alleged supernatural power of the pyramids. There are numerous alternative theories regarding pyramids, they are all grouped together in what is now called 'pyramidology'. Regardless of whether you subscribe to all or any of the various claims relating to pyramids and their power, I am sure you would agree that the points I have raised here are food for thought in respect to our past holding some hidden wisdom for us to draw upon.

There are many theories relating to the past, some which I openly admit to believing, and some that I secretly keep in my head. Personally, I believe that in times gone by, we held a far stronger belief in the unknown. I know this may come across as something of puzzle, but when it is all pieced together you may start to understand what I mean.

I believe Albert Einstein holds the key to the puzzle. His Theory of Relativity (the faster you travel through space, the slower you travel through time) was close to the mark in unlocking a lot of the mystery surrounding strange happenings many thousands of years ago. Even he, a genius, could not quite figure it all out. With that in mind, my theory may well be lambasted, but I do believe that we have a connection to our past, and that we can influence our future by connecting with the universe and becoming one with it, and drawing on the vast power reservoir available to us.

I know some of you will be fascinated by what I say, but that there will also be sceptics reading this. Perhaps they would have what I say ridiculed. I allow them this, and I do not oppose what they might say against my theories. Since Albert Einstein backs me up, I do not care.

The mind is the strongest tool we have to help us secure the riches within the universe. Before I take you on the journey to seek out those riches, I feel that I have to offer you every single chance of understanding what I write. Look at it this way, say you go shopping: you fill your trolley with all the goodies, and then you get to the checkout to find that your credit card is declined. Wouldn't you be angry? I want to make sure that your spiritual credit card is charged up with spending power, and that you can shop to your heart's content.

For some of you, what I have said might have gone over your heads. You might be speed-reading through this, scanning for the answers to what you want. Well that will not work, not in the long run. In the short term you might get lucky and have the odd success, but I put that down to beginners luck. I want to fill your pockets with money of a spiritual nature, and then you can spend, spend, spend and spend.

So please bear with me, as this is not a quick fix solution. The more desperate you are for it to work, the less success you might have. You do not need desperation, just the know-how and a few simple rules will do. 'Desperate times call for desperate measures'. So the cliché goes, but that is not the case here. I do not want this book to be your last-ditch bid to get rich, because it does not work like that, no matter how hard you try. By the same token, I am not saying you should be carefree, either.

I would ask you to use the theory of Pyramid Power as a symbol of what you can make happen for yourself. You may have heard the claim that pyramids act as antennas, reaching out into the universe. You may have also heard claims that blunt razor blades become self-sharpening when placed under a pyramid shaped cover overnight. Well, since I have never tried these experiments I cannot vouch for them, and I do not have any interest in finding out if they are true.

What I will say, though, is we can use the metaphorical value of the pyramid to psychologically help bolster our mental energy. Imagining that the geographic figure of the pyramid represents our head, the tip of the pyramid is the crown of our head. Imagine the base of the pyramid represents the four cardinal points at the base of our brain. That structure represents the field of mental energy we will use to help us visualise our wishes during relaxation.

Just as signals from mobile phones are said to be exerting pressure on our brains, so too do electromagnetic fields. Some of you living near pylons or other large electrical installations may need to relax and visualise while away from these electrical forces that can interfere with such exercises. Certain illness have been alleged to have stemmed from living near to pylons and other electrical installations, so perhaps this will tell you something. I do not want to start a mass exodus of people living near pylons, as these cancer theories are speculative. However, I do personally believe that these pylons could scramble your communication with the cosmos.

I know that this theory of mine might come across as implausible, but I have the scientific proof! Have you ever seen the Sunday newspaper magazine advertisements for machines that charge the air with negative ions? Let me tell you a little about ions: ions reproduce and repair body cells. They are transmitted into the body through the air, and are circulated by the blood. Some scientists claim that too many positive ions, the result of air pollution, can cause depression and sickness. Negative ions are attributed with having a beneficial effect on the body.

I believe Sick Building Syndrome is attributable to too many positive ions in the air, as well as the modern chemicals present in the build finish. Some modern buildings are a nightmare to be in. These new buildings are insulated from the outside world, with restricted airflow, hi-tech air conditioning systems pumping out all the electromagnetic energy, and desktop machinery whirring away all day long. Topped off by photocopier dust discharging itself into the air, and the way mobile phones and pagers are sending and receiving signals all day long, it is not surprising that Sick Building Syndrome is a very real thing. Sometimes when I enter a modern building, an invisible barrier hits me that no amount of feng shui can get rid of. When I walk out of them into the open air I feel like I have been released from a cloud of despair.

We are now seeing more people with allergies than ever before. Our modern, insular living has caused us to become walking catalogues of negativity. Similarly, the free minds we once possessed in the past have effectively been closed down by modern living, and we have lost the ability to connect with the universe.

I live in a house that is nearly 400 years old. I was drawn to it, the ions within it are negatively charged, and that is not a guess, I can feel it. My mind can operate in this sort of environment and it helps me connect me with the universe. The rooms have enormous windows and free flowing chimneys, all allowing for an easier connection with the cosmos.

Compare this to the place where you will be doing your relaxing and thinking. How can you visualise yourself driving the car of your choice in surroundings that restrict your messages from being heard? Arrange at least one room in such a way that your thoughts will not be interfered with. By all means listen to music – but taped, not the radio, as radio waves are going to get in the way. Sit by a window or some place that allows your thoughts to get out of the building.

Some of you live and work in the city. Imagine how you would feel sitting somewhere away from the hustle and bustle, a quiet thinking place. Being near nature helps, even one of those water features you can buy is a connection with the universe. If you have a garden, sit there, if it is away from prying eyes.

A good time to connect to the cosmos is after a heavy rainfall; even the air smells much purer than before. Just as a pyramid generates negative ions, so too can you create such an environment. There is no need to buy one of those negative ion-creating machines; a few simple steps taken by you can create an ambience conducive to cosmic communication. I do not expect you to go out and buy a pyramid shaped canopy to sit under. Although they are believed to have a generally balancing effect on the electromagnetic field of the body, why use such a contraption when your mind can do it all for you?

Some people like to have the psychologically enhancing use of a piece of quartz crystal, and some even go so far as to 'charge' them beneath a pyramid shaped cover. I recall how my friend, when he was alive, and I used to camp out near some old disused lead mines when we were teenagers. We used to go down the shafts of the safer-looking openings and collect fluorspar, the discarded leftovers dug out from the lead seams. These pieces of different coloured quartz were amazing to look at and hold. We would shout to each other in amazement when we discovered a large piece of quartz.

Personally, if something boosts you psychologically, then I would say that it is probably a good thing. So long as you feel positive about yourself, do whatever it takes. Even if it means carrying a rabbit's foot in your pocket, or sitting beneath a pyramid shaped housing (although I prefer the metaphorical use of the latter).

To pick a metaphor from everyday life, imagine that you are waiting for a particular bus. There is a large queue of people waiting, but you don't know if they are waiting for the same bus as you. A bus approaches; people crane their necks to see if it is their bus. The bus stops and some people alight and some people board it, but it is not yet your bus. You look at your watch in the hope that this helps materialise the bus, and you keep looking. You know that if the bus does not hurry up then you are going to be late for an appointment, so in your mind you will it to appear. And there, in the distance, looms your bus, and all your tension evaporates.

This is just the same as Cosmic Ordering. You are one of many people desiring a similar thing, but not necessarily exactly the same thing. There are enough things to go around for all of us, just like buses. Just as some people get on the bus, you see people all around you getting what they want. You see the ones alighting from the bus, who have had their dreams fulfilled.

Your own dreams stand alone, longing to be fulfilled, and you wonder if it will ever happen. You must have faith. Just as the bus was a little late, so too can fulfilment of your desires come a bit late. In fact, like buses, sometimes you wait around for ages and ages and then two turn up at the same time. When what you've requested of the cosmos comes to be, you feel relieved and kick yourself for having doubted it would turn up, as you knew in the back of your mind all along that it would.

When you are in a state of relaxation you can use this metaphor to help you realise your dream or ambition. Imagine that your dream request is on its way, and wait at the bus stop for the bus to bring it along to you. No matter how big the item you dream of, that bus will be carrying it. The bus pulls up and the item manifests itself. See yourself smiling as everything happens as you knew it would.

Even think in this way with your ambitions. Maybe you've always longed to be able to play the piano. The bus pulls up, you see six burly men unloading a piano and placing it on the ground. They beckon to you to come and sit down at the stool that they have placed in front of it. You oblige them, and as you flex your fingers, people stop what they are doing and gather around. You take your place at the piano, your fingers move over the keys with a mind of their own, and the most enchanting music on earth comes out. Everyone hearing the music you are creating stops in their tracks, awestruck. You finish your piece, take a bow, and everyone applauds you.

The examples I have given, or your own scenarios, can be used at any time. They are reinforcements meant to act as an aid to what I will teach you to do later on. These thoughts are rather like reminders of your dreams; you are reminding the cosmos to make your dreams become reality.

I am telling you this now because I want to get you into a positive train of thought for later on. A little practice beforehand will prepare you to run these thoughts effortlessly through your mind when connecting with the cosmos. There is no point in trying to formulate these thoughts while you are hooked up to the higher plain, you need a pre-prepared script. Just as an athlete will mentally run through specific actions before participating in a game or event, you will run through what you hope to achieve before connecting to the higher plane. How often have you watched sports on TV, or at an event, and seen world-class athletes performing all sorts of actions while deep in thought? They have practiced and thought about their movements so much that they are now second nature, and they can concentrate on using these moves to win the game.

You would not expect to go to, say, a rock concert and see the band playing air guitar. You can bet, though, that they have stood in front of a mirror umpteen times and practised their routines. What you see on stage is a polished performance, and that will be equally true of your performance. You will be able to rehearse and rehearse as often as you like, and when it comes to the actual performance you will be perfect.

Just imagine being able to fast track your cosmic order – using the power of your mind you can make it happen. Here is an exercise that will prove you can do it. After reading this instruction I would like you to close your eyes, but not before thinking of a cup. With your eyes closed, think again of that cup. Open your eyes when you have visualised it as clearly as you can.

Now that your eyes are open, describe that cup in as much detail as you can. Some of you will only be able to recall the shape of it. There is nothing wrong with that, don't worry. Some of you will recall the cup in great detail, perhaps able to talk about its unique design, colour, weight and even what was in it. Whatever you've described is fine, just so long as you actually imagined a cup.

Should you have shut your eyes and not been able to imagine a cup, then you would be part of a very small group of people who are not able to focus. There are mind exercises to help this condition, and I would advise you to look into these before trying to put what follows in this book to use. I sympathise with your plight if you failed to imagine a cup, but it does occasionally happen.

Now the 99.9 per cent of us can move on. But before I close this chapter I would like to run one more thing by you. Find a pen or pencil, you will not need paper. Before reading any further than the end of this paragraph, please write down five uses for a common building brick in the spaces numbered on the next page. If you do not have access to a pen or pencil (maybe you are on the beach, etc.), then just make a mental note, but do that now before reading any further.

1. House

2. Wall

3. Paving

4. Bookend

5. Hold down tarpauling / netting

Some of you will have read on to this paragraph without listing the uses for a brick, and that was part of the test! For those of you who read on without even bothering to look for a pen or pencil, you are going to need to apply a lot of effort to what follows. You will have to learn discipline of the mind. But I am pleased to say that you are now well on your way to obtaining that, as you will always remember this incident, subconsciously. For those of you who carried out my wishes, I congratulate you. You are the ones most likely to make a cosmic connection easily.

The fun part now is telling you something about yourself that you may not have known. If you listed uses along the lines of: a table for a dwarf; paint it a colour and use it as an ornament; hang it from string in the garden as a piece of sculpture, etc, then you are artistic. For those of you who wrote things like: use as a door stop; put under the wheel of your car to stop it rolling away; throw it through a window, etc., then you are not very artistic. Luckily, this does not make any difference to how well you will be able to connect to the cosmos; it was just a fun test.

6

United Field Theory

Ancient documents tell us that Jesus prayed to God to be spared from crucifixion as it was such an agonising way to die, but that his prayers fell on deaf ears and so he resigned himself to the excruciating death that lay ahead of him. When he died his body was put in a tomb, and eventually, Mary Magdalene was the first to see him rise from the dead.

Jesus, it is claimed, died for mankind. He was alleged to have been the Son of God, and now millions of people look to him as their saviour. All three: the Father, the Son and the Holy Ghost (Holy Spirit) join as one, united in heaven. God, according to the Scriptures, can and does fill simultaneously the two roles of Father and Holy Spirit, and is also manifest in the human form as Jesus ... united as one, yet all appearing to be singular.

Certainly I do not want to open a can of worms, as I am sure those with a deeper interest in such matters can give myriads of explanations. I am not going to pour cold water on that theory, as that is just what it is, essentially. As a result of the belief of what happened some 2,000 years ago, there are now some 2 billion people following Christianity as a faith. This is something I will leave to the atheist, the agnostic and the monolith to argue over.

My point, though, is that as the Father, the Son and the Holy Ghost conjoined to become one, so it is with United Field Theory. They become one. I have strayed from the norm by using the example of the Holy Trinity to demonstrate Albert Einstein's United Field Theory (UFT). His dream was to unite electromagnetism, gravity and space. It is a physical theory that combines the treatment of two or more types of fields in order to deduce previously unrecognised interrelationships, especially such a theory unifying the theories of nuclear, electromagnetic, and gravitational forces. The UFT, as used by Einstein, is an attempt to unify all the fundamental forces, and the interactions between elementary particles into a single theoretical framework. Einstein attempted to reconcile the general theory of relativity with electromagnetism in a single field theory.

As hard as Einstein tried, he failed to realise his dream of making the UFT a reality, which is sometimes called the Theory of Everything (TOE). And to this day, his quest has proved elusive to physicists. This holy grail of a UFT would explain the nature and behaviour of all matter.

Perhaps the answer to Einstein's quest was closer to hand than he could ever have imagined. Uniting the electromagnetic forces within us, and becoming one with the universe – this is creating a united field. Perhaps you are now beginning to understand the concept of Cosmic Ordering.

I have my own theory: ignorance is bliss. The less you know, the more confident you can be in tackling things. For instance, when we were children nothing seemed impossible. Then, as we grew out of childhood, we viewed the world through less confident, battle-scarred eyes. Well, just as you may know very little about what I am putting to you, then so it is that this ignorance is your saviour. You cannot get it wrong; you do not need to remember every single thing I am explaining within this guide. Just as I did when I started out as an ignorant hopeful, you too, armed with my help, will have your successes.

Recalling some of my first connections with the universe, I was masterfully ignorant. I believed all I had to do was direct my voice to the heavens and request whatever I wanted. In time, though, my learning and confidence grew, and nothing could make me lose sight of my goals. Some of my desires were granted, and looking back on it I am not astounded that it worked. My mind was tuned, and I had made my own United Field.

Then as I discovered more and more about what I was doing I set about things in a different way. I would add little extras into my connection technique, and out of the blue I was able to connect in a way I had never been able to. It was then that I realised that my past connections had been hit and miss, and how lucky I had been to connect with the cosmos at all.

Learning new techniques, and then using them and seeing them work gave me something I had never known – peace of mind. As long as I applied the laws of the universe to what I desired, I knew it would happen. This is something I will teach you in a later chapter, for the moment I want to influence the subconscious part of your mind. You do not even need to try to take in all of what I am directing at you. Just as you would not expect to be able to run a marathon without first training and becoming fit enough to complete the distance of 26 miles, so it is with grasping the techniques of Cosmic

Ordering. Look at these earlier chapters as a mind-tweaking exercise.

The essential belief of the UFT is that the four fundamental forces, as well as all matter, are simply different manifestations of a single fundamental field. They all essentially come from the same force, just as the Father, the Son and the Holy Ghost are one and the same. Shakespeare said, 'Nothing can be made out of nothing.' Well, if that is the case, how did the universe come about? The answer is: pure geometry. I do not want to baffle you with rocket science, so I will not expand greatly on that answer, which may even be beyond the comprehension of a rocket scientist.

Extrapolation from String Theory is the idea that our universe may have a twin universe that is only a subatomic distance away by an extra dimension. In physics, the forces between objects can be described as mediated by fields. The current theory says that at subatomic distances, quantum fields interacting, according to the laws of quantum mechanics, replace these fields. Which basically means the String Theory predicts possible extra dimensions of space-time.

The space we live in has three dimensions: height, width and depth. Another way to look at it is that we need three numbers to exactly locate ourselves on the Earth: longitude, latitude and elevation above sea level. However, when mathematicians or physicists talk about dimensions, they talk in a different language. The tradition is to label these three coordinates $(x, y$ & $z)$, with z usually denoting height. This is the case with what you will be doing, sending out signals as to your location. Just think, your desires go into a big melting pot, but where can they be delivered to you? This is my argument for those who have asked the cosmos for help – it is how you go about it that achieves results. We need to work on the theory that the delivery driver needs an address before he can deliver. You have to learn how to draw what you want to you, as opposed to making it happen for someone else.

One of the big discoveries of early classical physics was the similarity between the forces of gravity and electrostatic. This gives physicists an interesting way to do fine measurements of the numbers of dimensions of space. They can look at the gravitational force and put quantitative limits on any funny behaviour that would come from possible extra dimensions. We can use these gravitational pulls to our advantage. They will help draw the things you desire towards you, as if you were a magnet.

These extra dimensions of space are usually undetectable, or at least very difficult to detect by us, but they are there. They could be just an atom's distance away from us, yet we can co-exist without realising. And that is fact, quantum fact.

According to Isaac Newton, time was universal for all objects, no matter their motion relative to one another. This point of view held until Einstein turned it on its head. Einstein's Special Theory of Relativity, which makes classical mechanics consistent with classical electromagnetism, treats time like a coordinate in unified space-time geometry. Einstein's full theory of space-time, called general relativity, takes the concept of a four dimensional space-time and extends it to a curved space-time, where time and space make one united fabric that is curved and stretched and twisted by the distribution of matter.

I use Einstein's Special Theory of Relativity to support my own theory of Cosmic Ordering, and to becoming one with the universe and higher dimensional world. This, then, is what I believe to be the single mathematical framework in which all fundamental forces and units of matter can be described together, in a manner that is internally consistent, and consistent with current and future observation. We can become one with the universe, and it can happen with the greatest of ease.

Imagine playing a giant game of catch: you throw the ball billions of miles, billions of light years, and yet the ball need hardly leave your hand in order to reach the destination, as the destination is already there. In effect, we are playing a subatomic game of catch – don't blink or you will miss it. It is this momentum and energy between objects that will get you what you desire.

Just as a religious follower will send his or her prayers to their chosen one, so it is with Cosmic Ordering. You are sending a prayer; a spiritual connection is being made. You do not need to be a special person or possess special skills to make a connection. In fact, it is highly likely that you already possess the ability within you to get what you desire. I am not asking you to drop your religious beliefs, if you have any. You are not sending a prayer out to a god; you are connecting with the whole universe. Everything within the universe is drawn upon, and if there is a god within that universe then all the better for connecting to it. The religious approach is something you can use or discard, that is entirely your decision. You do need to understand how nature works in order to unify the fundamental forces and become one with the universe.

Going back to Einstein for a moment: he would have been an ideal candidate for Cosmic Ordering, as he had an unwavering belief in himself. For the last thirty years of his life, Einstein tried to find a theory that would do what Cosmic Ordering does. He had a deep faith that these forces were different manifestations of one and the same entity, thus demystifying the universe in a single set of equations.

The United Field Theory is what I was introduced to back in the Nineties. I thank my little Iranian friend for being so patient with me and my lack of ability to grasp what he was on about. To me, he might as well have spoken in Persian, or even tongues. I knew of his contentment, I knew of his moneymaking abilities, but I did not really, initially, pay any attention to his broken English and exaggerated facial movements that went in time with his windmill-like arm movements.

At times I used to sympathetically nod and smile at what he was saying, although I couldn't understand a word of it. Eventually I could understand him, and I even asked him to teach me some Persian. I used to drive around with Persian pop songs blasting out from my car stereo, as by this time I had given up riding my motorbike after a series of near-misses and nasty accidents. I had asked my friend to lend me some audiotapes in order to grasp the Iranian dialect, which is, at times, as guttural as German. My friend used to laugh at my poor attempt at speaking Persian, and my Western accent. I used to emphasise the guttural sounds, and nearly choke as I tried to pronounce names, etc.

Although I was aware of my friend's wealth, I automatically assumed he was connected to Iranian Royalty ... well I wasn't far wrong, but that is another story. I will go as far to say that he was a staunch supporter of the exiled Shah of Iran. When political allegiances changed he eventually came over to England, being of the Christian faith. This is where I will leave the politics to one side, as I do not have any political allegiance or agenda. I will also add that I do not have any affiliation to any specific religion, not even New Age. I accept all as they are, and I hope that you too will subscribe to that universal motto.

Over time we discussed many things: his upbringing in Iran, his departure from Iran, and his continuance to exist without state benefits. My friend was not one to rely on the state to support him. After arriving in England, with little but his memories of the old Iran, he had to start afresh. Speaking little English, somehow he made it.

After we became firm friends he started to open up and, with the use of further animated movements, facial gestures and guttural sounds, he managed to convey to me his belief in a higher intelligence. I must admit, I was still a bit of a philistine at that time, but I had sought religious help for my past problems, so this was something I thought worth giving a go.

Our bodies are made up of atoms, and every atom is a torsion generator, whether we like it or not. An atom is actually a vortex of aesthetic energy, where the negatively-charged electron clouds are pressing in towards the positively charged nucleus via the Biefield-Brown effect, but you need not trouble yourself over this. We will be harnessing those torsion waves to help boost our chances of success.

All matter harnesses torsion waves to sustain its existence. You read earlier on that geometry is a major factor in the quantum realm, since it represents the natural form that vibration creates in a fluid-like medium. Atoms will blend together into a larger whole, unifying and becoming one. The key to this is vibration. In order for this vibration to occur, an atom must be constantly absorbing and radiating aesthetic energy at the same time. As this vibration continues, the atom will throw off torsion waves into the surrounding ether. This means that every atom is a torsion generator. Just as passing electric current through a coil of wire generates an electrostatic or electromagnetic field, you will also produce measurable torsion waves.

I do not hypothesise about what I write. The Institute of Material Research determined that people with strong psychic abilities were also capable of creating identical changes in the spin polarisation of various substances by the sheer focus of their consciousness. No other known technology could create such changes in a physical object. Remember, knowledge is power.

7

Making the Cosmic Connection

Why wait for the winning lottery number, when by following my guidance you will find you can achieve almost anything? Remember, there can only be a few big winners per lottery draw, maybe even just one. It would not be possible for the cosmos to grant every single request for a lottery win; there are just not enough winning tickets to go around.

Up till now I have been using subliminal suggestion and embedded commands that bypass your conscious reasoning and speak directly to the subconscious mind to help you achieve an unconscious understanding of how to make the cosmic connection. My doing this will allow you to take specific actions without having to apply a great deal of effort.

Without any effort, your subconscious mind runs on autopilot. I have been feeding it unusual patterns of language that force the subconscious mind to wake up and pay attention. Maybe now you know why you became somewhat awakened when reading certain parts of this guide, and became somewhat drowsy, perhaps feeling a little detached, when reading other parts. If that happened, then that was my intention, and things are working in your subconscious. I would not expect to see a reaction to these embedded commands until you are ready to put them into action. I hope you agree that this is the best way forward in helping you get what you want.

Before qualifying as a clinical hypnotherapist I qualified as a counsellor. My job involved helping people who were suffering from various psychological disorders. The first rule of being a counsellor is to accept people with unconditional regard, to accept them as they are. No matter how minor or how serious their problem, I would always go at their pace. The same applies here; everything is at your pace. There is no hurry; wait until you feel ready to make the first positive move towards ordering yourself a better life. You will know when the time is right. We have one thing in common, we are all different.

I would not expect anyone who has suffered a recent close bereavement to suddenly snap out of it and form a positive frame of mind. Equally so if you feel totally down at the moment – clinical depression is something that can come and go. Certainly this guide will still be of some use though, even if only in a spiritual way, to anyone wishing to achieve success. Just by reading it your life will have progressed forward.

I recall reading about how busy executives would have a 'clear hour'. They would put a notice on their door or desk, and everyone working with them agreed not to disturb them during this time. You will find this to be of great help to you, as it is distracting to be disturbed during the time you will be relaxing. Of course, you will not need an hour.

The first thing you must ask yourself is do you live to work or work to live? We all have our unfulfilled dreams and ambitions. From this moment on you are in charge of your own destiny. I am excited at the prospect of you making good things happen in your life, and you too should feel the same surge of expectancy.

To begin with I will take you through this initial period of expectancy with as little fuss as possible. Later on I will show you how you can make some great things happen. Right now, as you read this, I would like you to follow what I say.

- Close your eyes and run through your head all of the things you have ever dreamed of wanting, no matter how outrageous. When you are finished, open your eyes and start reading again. Do that now, close your eyes.

- Now I want you to have a clear out, and get rid of all the physically impossibly goals. Obviously, if you are a male, you might be too old to become a UK Premiership League soccer player or to play in the American Super Bowl. Similarly, if you are female, you might not be able to give birth at the age of 70.

- After having cleared the unobtainable from your wish list, I want you to think of the three most-likely-to-be-obtained things that you want. You can leave your eyes open for this one, if you want.

- You have now started to bring the creative part of your mind to play. What are the three most important achievable things you want? Put the wish list in order of importance, and now you have something to aim for.

- Now, simply find some place where you can spend a few quiet moments to think of nothing but these things. Once there, you need do nothing more than ask the cosmos to make them happen. Obviously you can say these things in your mind or aloud, whichever you feel comfortable with.

- You can address the cosmos however you wish, 'Dear Cosmos, I ask you to replace my old, faithful car with a newer and better model. I want a ...'

- Remember, ordering has a beginning, middle and an end: you see what you want, you go for it, and then think about the advantages of having it.

- Be specific about what you want. For instance, specify that you want the car to be delivered to your address, even ask for it to be yours within the next few weeks.

- Now visualise the car parked at your door; or the new three-piece suite actually sitting in your home; or that painting you always wanted – see it hanging on your wall.

- Finish off your thoughts or words with a 'thank you'. Always thank the cosmos. Do not cajole it!

There you are, you have ordered from the cosmos, simple as that. Remember, we are all connected to the universe, and you have tapped into something that is fundamentally as secure as bars of gold bullion in the world money market.

Now that you have made your requests, you should have an air of expectancy. You will not ever have one shred of doubt about it happening or manifesting itself.

Sometimes things can go AWOL, and you will wonder, 'why hasn't it happened?' Look around you. Have you had doubt? Has your neighbour, somehow, ended up with your new car? Always have positive thoughts – it is no good wishing for a new car and then worrying if the car will be on finance, with crippling repayments. Rid yourself of any such negative thoughts. Doubtful thoughts can come back to haunt you. Always feel worthy of what you wish for. Just as Einstein had an unwavering belief in himself, so you too must believe in yourself. I will tell you a story that I hope will illustrate what belief is.

A little boy was out with his parents, visiting friends at a summer barbeque. The friends had a swanky house with a large, inviting swimming pool.

The little boy asked his father, 'Dad, if I jump in the pool would you jump in after me and get me out?'

The boy's father replied, 'Of course, son.'

Without warning the little boy jumped into the deep end of the pool.

After the father had dived in and pulled the boy out to safety he asked his son, 'Why did you jump in, you know you can't swim?'

The boy replied with unwavering certainty, 'Because you said you would jump in and get me out, Dad.'

Now that is unwavering belief, the kind you have to develop within yourself. This is not a book about building up your self-confidence, and it is not an ego-boosting book. I would advise anyone with a lack of self-confidence to go and buy one of those types of book, or even go for a hypnotherapy session with a qualified clinical hypnotherapist. Please remember, though, that not everyone is a candidate for hypnotherapy.

It is not within the scope of this book to boost your confidence. That would take at least another book of the same size. By the same token, I am not saying you must be overly confident, as this too can be a problem. You can be blinded into believing that you can walk on water. You must be realistic in your beliefs. You would not, I hope, take up the challenge of going over Niagara Falls in a barrel, as this would be a foolish and dangerous thing to do. You cannot challenge the laws of nature, so be careful.

This chapter has given you the basic principles to build on, and in a later chapter I will take you on to the advanced cosmic connection principle. For now just close the book, if you wish, and let your subconscious mind continue to send those signals to the cosmos, even while you sleep.

I know that reading books can be of great therapeutic value. Those books are for your leisure time; this book is for your future. Do not self-destruct by trying to cram it all into your head at once; you will only end up with mental burn out. There will be times when you have to devote at least half an hour from your hectic schedule to these principles; can you afford not to give the time? Remember, you sometimes cannot make it happen within a day, miracles can take a little longer.

Have you ever heard the story about the grasshopper and the squirrel? Through the summer the squirrel gathers a store of nuts, hiding them in readiness for winter. The grasshopper, by stark contrast, just jumps about and enjoys itself. When winter arrives, the grasshopper has nothing to eat, but the squirrel has a stash of nuts to survive on.

Just as the squirrel invested time in itself so that it could survive the winter, you will have to collect your fair share of proverbial nuts. You have to think about the future. The future is the next minute, not tomorrow. Start investing in yourself now, spend that little extra time every now and again on bolstering your belief in yourself, and in doing so being able to gain what you have wished for.

Do not allow negative thoughts or jealousy to get in the way of your visualisation techniques. Imagine yourself with the goods or situation you wish for. There is no need to keep asking the cosmos for the same thing, but gentle and subtle reminders can, and do, help the process along.

I know of one millionaire who kept images of what he desired stuck to his fridge door. He eventually obtained all of those things and more. Remind yourself of your goals and wishes; do not let them fall by the wayside in the hope that one day they might happen. They will happen.

8

Cosmic Confidence

You may recall my earlier words that it was not within the scope of this book to give an ego-boost to those with low self-esteem. However, I can give you some guidance in focusing your thoughts on securing what you want.

For some of you, chasing your dreams and securing the fruits of your effort is going to be a labour of love. You will be able to nurture your cosmic connection and hone your skills to the point where it just happens. I do not want to dash your hopes and dreams, as they are sacred to you, but there may be times when you encounter obstacles, maybe even cosmic objections.

Your messages may encounter crossed wires and be received at the other end with a different meaning, rather like Chinese whispers. A story that eloquently lends itself as an example is the one of a radio message, sent during WWII, from the army fighting on the Front Line to battle headquarters (HQ). The radio operator was told by the colonel to ask HQ for help.

The radio operator spoke to HQ with the colonel's request: 'Send reinforcements, we're going to advance.'

Back at HQ, the radio operator, with a baffled look on his face, reported to the general. 'General,' he said, as he gulped for air, 'the Front Line have asked us to send three and four pence, as they are going to a dance.'

I hope that example will encourage you not to give up in despair, as misunderstandings can happen. Let me give you my own example. I asked the cosmos for some radio publicity for a project I was working on. Within a few days I received an unsolicited email from the USA. The sender of the email worked for a large American publicity machine who wanted to act for me in securing radio interviews in the USA and Canada. 'Great!' I thought. I was working on a book called *Psycho Stephen* (about Stephen Moyle). The book covered how Stephen skipped bail whilst waiting to be sentenced in England on firearms charges. After running away to Canada, Stephen was going to swim the treacherous Niagara River in order to get across into America. So I thought this was a great opportunity for me to plug the book on Canadian radio. The only problem was, the company that had emailed me wanted payment for securing their services, to the tune of US$10,000!

I had been granted my request for a radio interview, as I had asked, but at a very steep price. I then rephrased my request and included the word 'free' within it. But I still thanked the cosmos for granting me what I had asked for. The point is, be careful how you word your requests. Oh, and that free radio interview ... I eventually secured it.

Another great story shows how people can be talking, but not communicating. The now dead and legendary oil well trouble-shooter Red Adair was brought in to cap an oil well that had burst free. After days of spurting the rich, black bullion into the air, a cap was fitted by one of Red Adair's associates, but the oil just kept on pumping through it. Red was called in personally, and the flow was staunched.

'The problem,' Red said, was miscommunication between his men. Apparently, 'the cap had been put on upside down. It was,' he continued, 'a case of them talking, but not communicating.'

With this example in mind, do communicate your needs to the cosmos in a way that is not misinterpreted as something else.

I know that some of you reading this will have a constant stream of everyday tasks. For some of you, living is a busy business, even if it is doing what you love. The myriad of everyday tasks can become time consuming chores, they can become a burden, and this can dishearten you. This is when some of you may give up in despair.

In between these endless chores there may be periods when you feel that there are insurmountable hurdles to overcome, and you can easily get caught up and distracted from your main goals. These distractions can act physically to block your thoughts and connections with the cosmos. They can drain your spiritual energy until you find that all you are emitting are negative thoughts.

Your thoughts have to be re-focused to what you want to have manifested in front of you. You might have tried and tried, and gotten to the point where you feel that your requests are not being heard, that your dreams are unreachable. Your negative thoughts can mean that your subconscious is sending out the wrong message, maybe even a mixed message of strange requests. How can you get what you want if deep down you know you are not going to get it?

If you find that you are at this point, then I can help you re-focus your spiritual energy, and overcome the stumbling block. You can keep your vision alive by using some simple techniques, and by doing so you will, with a renewed passion, charge your subconscious with positive signals.

Let me tell you, I was once so full of negativity that it would have taken a whole life-sized pyramid of power to turn it around for me into positive energy. Before I even started anything, I knew that I would fail. I would drive into town, but I knew I would get caught up in every traffic jam there ever was, and sure enough I did. Things got so messed up that I would not even start to do things for fear of being unable to accomplish them, and ending up in tears. I only had negative vision, and as a consequence my spirit was broken.

Still, during my periods of despair, while carrying out the chores of everyday life, I would catch glimpses of my dreams. I would see a luxury car driving past me, and wish it were in my possession. Just as fast as the car passed me by, my dream would vanish. The very passion the car had evoked in me was short-lived; negativity had dashed my dreams against the rocks of despair.

Now, though, I know how to keep that passion alive, how to keep that anticipation within me, even while going about my everyday activities. They say that Julius Caesar, the Roman Emperor, could do five things at once, and that is just how you will be able to do things. Today they call it 'multi-tasking'. You will be able to simultaneously deal with the day-to-day tasks, while keeping an eye on your visions. Just as you might write a checklist when you go shopping, or when you pack your holiday suitcase, you might want to write one to remind yourself of your needs. That checklist will become an aid-memoir to what you want. That is how you can keep your vision alive without undue effort. That shopping list might not even come out of your pocket during your trip to the shop, because you have already reinforced your needs into your mind by writing them down.

Before you wrote the list, or as you were writing it, you thought about what you wanted. You probably checked the fridge or food cupboards to see what you needed to stock up on. Those actions were focusing your thoughts on your needs. Do the same with your life. Run through the cupboards of your mind, check what you need to stock up on, and then add a few luxury items to your mental notes. That checklist will come in handy. Even though you might not need to refer to it, it has prepared you mentally.

Have you ever been in love? I mean for the first time? If you have had numerous relationships then you know that, generally, during the initial stages of the romance, you are both constantly reassuring each other of your love. To show you what I mean, let's say that you have been with your partner for a number of years. If, during the first year of that relationship, you were to put a pin in a cushion every time you shared carnal pleasure with each other, just imagine how many pins there might be. After that first year, for every time you have carnal pleasure, remove a pin. For most couples, the reality is that it might take many years to remove the first year's worth of pins.

Just as you were passionate about your new love, so must you be passionate about your cosmic connections. You must keep your hopes alive, and get as many pins into that cosmic cushion of connections as you can achieve during your first impassioned and successful periods.

Turn your thoughts around. Instead of thinking of the things you do not have, think of the things you want. Woeful thoughts can hinder your positive vision. Certainly, cash is king; it allows you to have all of the material things you ever wanted. A lack of cash can turn your mind to negative thoughts, and without cash, things will not change. A better job means better pay, better holidays, contentment, luxury cars, a better home, etc. Use your positive thoughts to draw all of the things you want to you. Magnetise your mind with positive images and strong intentions. Discard feelings of despair, you want only feelings of hope.

Some people are born worriers – fact or fiction? Work it out for yourself. Stop yourself during the course of the day; get to know your mind. Do not let negative thought processes become second nature, or they will run on and on without you even noticing. Worrying can become automatic, and without your being aware of it, your thoughts can destroy your will to win. By stopping at certain points of the day and taking stock of your thoughts, you will know what you are running low on, and you can stock up on those positive thoughts. Empty your mind of the very things that will stop you getting what you want.

By all means, take positive advice from people, helpful guidance can never go amiss. As helpful guidance can boost your confidence, negative, scathing, remarks can damage it. Take a look at the person casting these negative things at you. What is missing from their life that makes them so bitter? You certainly know you do not want to end up like them. Use that person as an example of what you do not want to be. Soon you will be mixing with positive, like-minded people. The doubters and shirkers will soon be forgotten.

Put your attention on what you want, not what you have not got. Soon your thought processes will have changed, and you will become an Olympic champ of positive thinking. Listen to your mind, detect where the habitual negative thoughts are hidden. Sometimes these thoughts can be overpowering – you only want positive thoughts.

I do not expect you to sit in front of a mirror surrounded by candles while chanting mantras, making *ohmmming* sounds and ringing bells. Admittedly, it works for some, but it is a long-winded way to peace, and it does not always work. Perhaps you have already dabbled in incense sticks and aromatherapy; fine, I am not going to knock it. Even if carrying a rabbit's foot and a four-leaf clover around makes you feel confident, I am not going to advise against it, so long as it makes you feel positive.

In ancient times, when opposing armies battled with each other, a flag would be carried ahead of the army. When the flag bearer fell, someone else would come along and take charge of it. The flag was a symbol that united the soldiers; without the flag they would think that the battle was lost. Similarly, carry your own metaphorical flag, or four-leaf clover, in the form of positive thoughts. As long as the flag of hope is flying, then your positive thoughts will remain with you. Do not let your flag fall.

There will be times when you need to reinforce your positive thoughts. Do not think to yourself, 'I am fat'. Think, 'I want to be slim'. Run visions of yourself lying on the beach in some exotic location, or of you running in a 'fun run'. See how good you would look with a few pounds off you.

This positive imaging can be used in any given situation. Imagine yourself living in that better house. Imagine yourself driving that open-topped sports car. Imagine yourself in all sorts of wonderful situations. See how much better it makes you feel about yourself. Ditch the 'fat pig' sticker on the fridge; that is negative imaging, and it will destroy your positive imaging. Get rid of anything that calls up negativity or makes you feel bad about yourself. Throw out those old clothes that do not fit you anymore, as you are going to get more fashionable clothes when you have lost those extra pounds. Only have positive images around you, images of what you want to be, not what you do not want to be. Always be prepared to laugh at yourself, laugh off those worries and be happy.

Just as I have said that there is nothing wrong with carrying a four-leaf clover, equally, some people write what are called affirmations. For every negative thought, a positive thought is written down to counter it. Say you want success with something, an idea or a project, and you have had misgivings about it. You can write down what is good about it and why people want it to happen, thus turning negativity to your advantage. Whatever it takes to make you feel confident then that is worth doing.

These affirmations are just another positive imaging idea, an aid-memoir to your goals and dreams. You can do this with any negative thought. Some people believe that to make it work you have to write each affirmation down about a dozen times throughout the day. I would say that is a little obsessive, but, certainly, it would help reinforce your positive thoughts and would not harm you. Personally, I think that once you have written it, you will always be reminded of it, so there is no need to constantly write it out throughout the day. Should it make you feel better, write one affirmation per day, until you have no more negative thoughts left to write down. Exhaust your worries, and they will soon leave you.

There is another way you improve your self-esteem and start to turn your life around for the better, thus enhancing your cosmic thoughts. Sometimes I used to use what is called an 'open eyed' hypnosis technique (invented by David Grove, also called Groverian Therapy) when sending my hypnotherapy patients into trance. I would use this technique when the trauma they were trying to overcome was severe, perhaps in emotive matters such as the patient having suffered sexual abuse. By use of epistemological metaphors I could help empower the patient with tools to overcome their trauma. This technique would go into detail about their symptoms. They would be asked if they had any feelings about their situation. What did it feel like? Did it have a size, a shape or a colour?

After carrying out certain preliminary hypnosis-inducing procedures, the patient would be in trance with their eyes open! I would be able to find out from them what it was they were experiencing. Perhaps it felt like a knot in the stomach, or a pounding in the head, or a tightening of the throat. Just as they felt those symptoms when being abused, so they felt them now, when they had low self-esteem or felt worried.

You worriers will know what I am on about here, as you will have experienced many of those feelings. I certainly did as a child when I was bullied. A feeling of butterflies in my stomach would often precede being bullied. Perhaps I had even brought the bullying on by these feelings; maybe these feelings went hand-in-hand with the bullying.

It got to the point where I was giving myself nightmares because of this. Things got so bad that I even used to truant from school. I sat in a park for three weeks, during school time, until my mother caught me sitting there in the middle of a green. I look back on that now, at the frozen persona of a little boy that I was. I was so worried, not knowing what life was all about. I couldn't talk to my mother about it, and I couldn't run away. But eventually I learned how to combat and overcome these feelings, and you too will be able to do the same.

These negative physical feelings are messages from your subconscious, which is how it deals with the worry within you. All sorts of feelings can be attributed to a lack of confidence: a sinking feeling, tightening of the chest, a gripping feeling around the throat, losing the ability to speak, irritable coughs, a band around the head, a knot in the stomach, etc.

I can show you positive ways to overcome these feelings of despair, these messages from your subconscious. By clearing away these feelings you will have a recharged subconscious and will be able to direct your vision to the cosmos without allowing negative thoughts to intrude on your life.

Obviously there is not enough room within this book to go into sufficient detail to help those who are still suffering posttraumatic disorder from sexual abuse. For those of you who are unable to part from those feelings, I would advise that you seek out a professional clinical hypnotherapist specialising in Groverian Therapy. I can assure you, with this technique you would not even need to tell the hypnotherapist the cause of your trauma.

During the session, or sessions, you would not need to relive the trauma that so haunts you now. Sometimes just writing down these negative feelings, or trying to mentally shelve them, does not help to rid you of them.

Remember feelings relating to happiness: those warm glows that filled your cheeks, the happy stomach pains from laughing fits, and the tears of joy that would fall from your eyes. Think about these joyful feelings whenever you get the feelings of doubt about your body. If you are sick to the pit of your stomach with worry, then allow your stomach to feel the pains of laughter. Use your memories of happier times to wipe out those negative feelings. Do not sit slumped forward, pull your back up straight and feel good, you are alive.

Remembers the words of the song, 'smile, although your heart is aching', or something along those lines. You probably already know that it takes more facial muscles to frown than it does to smile, so smile away those worries. No one likes a misery guts. People will like you because you offer them a smile, a worry free smile. Before long, you will actually be able to smile genuinely. Of course, do not walk around with a smile etched permanently across your face, as this can scare people off. You will soon learn that a smile can win you a lot of friends. You will radiate warmth.

I do have a very personal recommendation on making negative thoughts evaporate, but it is a little risky. I do not mean medically risky, I mean embarrassingly risky. Use an audiotape to record your positive thoughts, perhaps, for instance, something along the lines of: 'My roses will win me first prize in the summer show, I know my roses are the best, as I am a great gardener, I was born with green fingers.'

Use whatever it takes to channel your positive thoughts into the recorder, and when you have some spare time you can play it back and let those positive thoughts flood through your mind. There is a subliminal way you can do this also, which is to play the tape when you are going to sleep. Perhaps you have recorded all of your positive, affirming, thoughts onto one cassette; great ... enjoy the sleep. You will awaken with a positive mind, and will be better able to dispel those negative thoughts.

The advice within this chapter should have put you in a positive phase, which is going to help you to realise your dreams. You should have an air of expectancy about you, or be working on developing such a state of mind. You can be certain that this positive state of mind and self-confidence will enhance your connection with the cosmos. You requests will be heard crystal clear, and you can expect to soon be getting what you want out of life and others.

When you feel up to it and have a level of confidence that allows it, tell your friends of your dreams. Mix with people who have made it happen for them; join the local operatic society or golf club, etc.

Should anyone try to knock your confidence by dispelling your dreams, avoid them. Ask your friends what their dreams are, and talk to them about yours. In fact, live the dream and it will become reality. Always accept, with thanks, the good things people say about you and your dreams.

When things come along to defeat you, they may sidetrack you for a moment, but that is all they will do. Get up and dust yourself off. You know things could be worse, and you will be able to defeat and beat these gremlins. Always be thankful for what you have, even though you know you will get more, and better, things. Difficulties are simply sent to test your mettle. Life never runs smoothly, that is life.

The following are positive affirmations that I would like you to mentally say to yourself on a daily basis:

- I persistently think and act in the direction of my good and my goal; to be a happy, healthy, relaxed person.
- I create my own reality through the power of my mind, and this is so.
- Negative thoughts have no power over me, I am in control.
- Every day, in every way, I am getting better and better.
- I am in control, I create my own reality.
- I am loving, loved and beloved.

What is important is how you face those setbacks that you will encounter; with a positive mind you can overcome any hurdle. The more people you have rooting for your success, the more likely that it will happen.

9

The Cosmic Eye

Up to this point I have been preparing you for something far more advanced than you may have ever thought possible ... the ultimate cosmic connection, the cosmic G-spot, so to speak.

Your mind should now be firmly focused on what you desire in life. It should not be something you have to consciously think of, it should be embedded within your subconscious. Now, before we move on to the next chapter, I want to concentrate on placing some pretty important embedded commands into your subconscious. The good thing about this particular chapter is that you do not even have to try and remember the contents. You can, if you want, read it whilst the TV is on or whilst doing something equally safe and similar.

Just allow yourself to absorb what is within this chapter, as though it is charging you with untold amounts of energy. Without any effort, just let these words enter the creative part of your mind. You may recall having read of the pineal gland, the cosmic eye, and its purpose. Those words are going to come in very handy in making the next stage happen – activating your cosmic eye.

Two important ingredients in developing the third eye are: imagination, and visualisation. Through the ages we have lost touch with our intuition, but this can be enhanced through cosmic eye development. When you are in full waking consciousness, memories of your visit to the cosmos will not completely register. You may have flashes of what went on, but not until your intuition becomes strong enough will such connections be fully recalled. You may not even be aware of a connection at first. Only good thoughts will flow from you. With increasing practice and use, the cosmic eye will become activated to a greater degree.

The pineal gland corresponds with divine thought after being touched by the vibrating light created within the head, and then starts its ascent towards the head centre. The light is located at the top of the soul thread, the thread that connects you to the cosmos. This invisible thread passes down from the highest plane of our being into the physical vehicle. The cosmic eye, the organ of spiritual vision, has become dulled in the natural course of evolution. As human beings continue to evolve, on the journey from spirit to matter, and back to spirit, the pineal gland will continue to rise from its state of age-long dormancy, bringing back to humanity astral capacities and spiritual abilities.

At certain brainwave frequencies, your sense of ego boundary will vanish. In the theta state, you are resting deeply and still conscious, but just at the threshold of conscious awareness. As your brain enters deeper states, your consciousness is less concerned with the physical state. Your cosmic eye will be activated, and a cosmic connection will become natural. Your self-identity will not hamper you; all constraining, mundane, conscious thought will leave you.

Many native traditions and mystical practices refer to the ability of the cosmic eye, or being aware of energy fields at higher levels. This new awareness is much more subjective and does not involve the normal level of mundane consciousness, which is mostly concerned with self-identity.

All senses of ego and personality are set aside; the consciousness is raised from an emotional nature into an illumined awareness when the pineal gland is lifted from its dormancy. When your sense of ego and personality are set aside, your mental energy will remain intact. You will be able to focus on your inner self, the subconscious, through different practices that activate the 'light in the head'.

The brain stem is the oldest and smallest region in the evolving human brain. It is at the base of your skull emerging from your spinal column, evolved hundreds of millions of years ago, and is similar to the entire brain of present-day reptiles. For this reason, it is often called the 'reptilian brain'.

Various clumps of cells in the brain stem determine the brain's general level of alertness and regulate the involuntary processes of the body, such as breathing, heart rate, and the fight or flight mechanism. Its impulses are instinctual and ritualistic. It is concerned with fundamental needs such as survival, physical maintenance, hoarding, dominance, preening, and mating. The basic ruling emotions of love, hate, fear, lust, and contentment emanate from this first stage of the brain.

Over millions of years of evolution, layers of more sophisticated reasoning have been added upon this foundation. If someone says that they reacted with their heart instead of their head, what they really mean is that they conceded to their primitive emotions, as opposed to the calculations of the rational part of the brain.

The brain is an electrochemical organ, using electromagnetic energy to function. Electrical activity emanating from the brain is displayed in the form of brainwaves. There are four categories of brainwaves: high amplitude, low frequency delta, low amplitude, and high frequency beta.

Men, women, and children of all ages experience the same characteristic brainwaves. They are consistent across cultures and country boundaries. During meditation brain waves alter. Examples of the types of brainwaves given off during various activities are:

- **BETA** – 13-30 cycles per second – waking awareness, extroversion, concentration, logical thinking, active conversation. A debater would be in high beta. A person making a speech, a teacher, or a talk show host would all be in beta when they are engaged in their work.
- **ALPHA** – 7-13 cycles per second – relaxation times, non-arousal, meditation, hypnosis.
- **THETA** – 4-7 cycles per second – daydreaming, dreaming, creativity, meditation, paranormal phenomena, out-of-body experiences, ESP, shamanic journeys. A person who is driving on a motorway, and discovers that they cannot recall the last five miles, is often in a theta state. It is a state where tasks become so automatic that you can mentally disengage from them. The ideation that can take place during the theta state is often free flow and occurs without censorship or guilt. It is typically a very positive mental state.

- **DELTA** – 1.5-4 or less cycles per second – deep dreamless sleep.

Using new scanning techniques, neuroscientists have discovered that certain areas of the brain light up constantly in Buddhists, which indicates positive emotions and good moods. Not that I am advocating any personal preference to any specific religious denomination when I make this remark. However, it scientifically proves that such activity in the brain does take place, and, therefore, that it is also possible for you to make it happen. The studies done by scientists at the University of Wisconsin at Madison showed activity in the left prefrontal lobes of experienced Buddhist practitioners. The area is linked to positive emotions, self-control and temperament.

I also cite research by Paul Ekman, of the University of California San Francisco Medical Centre, when he suggests that meditation and mindfulness can tame the amygdala, an area of the brain that is the hub of fear memory. Given what Ekman discovered, that experienced Buddhists are less likely to be shocked, flustered, surprised, or made angry as other people; it goes to reason that this state of mind is also attainable by you.

To further prove my point, a report in *New Scientist* magazine suggested that a reasonable hypothesis would be that there is something about conscientious Buddhist practice that results in the kind of happiness we all seek. I would add a caveat to that by saying that it is, in fact, the state of mind that makes this happen.

Scientists also discovered, after investigating the effect of the meditative state on Buddhist monks' brains, that portions of the organ previously active became quiet, whilst pacified areas became stimulated. Dormant areas in your brain can also awaken and allow that cosmic connection through your cosmic eye. Religion and spirituality can become one, whatever your religious denomination.

According to Andrew Newberg, a radiologist at the University of Pennsylvania, USA, we are 'poised at a wonderful time in our history to be able to explore religion and spirituality in a way which was never thought possible.'

Brain scans on Tibetan Buddhist monks as they meditated for approximately one hour produced some remarkable results. Newberg and his team asked the monks in the study to pull a kite string to their right, which released an injection of a radioactive tracer, when they reached a transcendental high. By injecting a tiny amount of radioactive marker into the bloodstream of a deep meditator, the scientists soon saw how the dye moved to active parts of the brain.

Later, when the monks had finished meditating, the regions were imaged and the meditation state compared with the normal waking state. The scans provided remarkable clues about what goes on in the brain during meditation.

Dr Newberg explained, 'There was an increase in activity in the front part of the brain, the area that is activated when anyone focuses attention on a particular task.'

Just as you will focus on requesting what you desire of the cosmos, so will your brain become activated to make that cosmic connection. And as I earlier in this book used the words 'time' and 'space', you may, during your connection, experience a sense of no space and time. There will be a notable decrease in activity in the back part of the brain, or parietal lobe, which is the area responsible for orientation. This reinforces the general suggestion that meditation leads to a lack of spatial awareness.

These feelings can be compared to being in deep prayer, for those of you who are religious. You have heard the expression 'my prayers have been answered'; this is also going to true of your cosmic connection.

Your connection is a spiritual prayer to the cosmos; it should be equally as moving as a deeply religious experience is for believers in their chosen religion. In fact, if we are to believe science, the complex interaction between different areas of the brain also resembles the pattern of activity that occurs during other so-called spiritual or mystical experiences.

There is a difference to what you will be doing, though. Prayers are usually offered verbally, which activates the attention area of the brain, and diminishes activity in the orientation area. In a deeper connective state you will have no need to use verbal requests. Your space and your time are sacred to you, and you alone.

Using powerful brain imaging technology, researchers are exploring what mystics call 'nirvana', and what Christians describe as a 'state of grace'. Scientists are asking whether spirituality can be explained in terms of neural networks, neurotransmitters and brain chemistry. It has been suggested that it could be the decreased activity in the brain's parietal lobe that creates that transcendental feeling of being one with the universe.

Some people believe strongly that religion has changed their lives, prompting divine feelings of love and compassion. Perhaps because spiritual practices activate the temporal lobe, which weights experiences with personal significance. Examining this in detail reveals that the brain has deep-seated leanings towards spiritual and religious experiences. Because of this, you are already primed to make that cosmic connection happen.

Knowing that the brain is predisposed to religion and spirituality, then might it be that God is a creation of the brain? Could it be that there is no God as such, but that there is a cosmos? Might that theory offend believers and reinforce atheistic views and, as a consequence, make religion appear useless?

Some scientists readily say that research proves there is no such thing as God. But many others argue that they are religious themselves, and that they are simply trying to understand how our minds produce a sense of spirituality. Having a spiritual experience makes you feel at one with the universe and you lose your singular sense of self. You lose that boundary between the self and the rest of the world. In doing so you are in a universal state.

When religious people talk of religious experience, they are talking of meditative experience. Hinduism and Buddhism both emphasise the importance of meditation and its power to make an individual loving and compassionate. Most Buddhists are disinterested in whether God exists.

Some religious beliefs involve commitments, suffering and struggle; it's not all meditative bliss. There are moments when the believer can feel abandoned by

God. In contrast to this, you will never have such commitments, suffering and struggles with a cosmic connection. You are free to believe in whatever you want to, without fear of rejection.

Already the biological processes of mankind are changing, bringing about the return of heightened sense capacity, and self-reflective consciousness. This is a return to the sacred domain of our inner technology.

Time as we know it is manmade, but we can regain our conscious connection to natural time in the universe when we make that cosmic connection. The human race has lost its way, to some extent, and now you are on the path to finding the right way.

Mankind seems to have a fatalistic tendency to make their ending come sooner rather than later, but now we have a chance to turn all of that primitive savagery and aggressiveness around. The technically highly developed society of today finds itself in a deep moral-ecological crisis. There are no simple ways out of this, but you are on the right pathway to making those changes happen by allowing a connection between science and religion. Even if that religion is proclaimed as New Age.

I have given you the scientific proof of how states of mind can change during such connections by citing scientific research, and I have given you a sense of belief that you can make that cosmic connection by activating your third eye. Certainly, stick bits of paper all over the house with your requests and needs written on them. Throw them to the four winds if it will help. But I am showing you a way that can accelerate your requests by making that connection direct, instead of by snail mail.

Already you have subconsciously mapped out your life, and your plans were formulated many years ago.

I know someone who always wanted a cosy relationship, wanted to escape their torrid times. This person wanted a little house, with a yard big enough for a line to hang their washing from. Unbeknownst to them, they had already preordained this to happen, and so it did.

This advanced planning is the same with your life. You may have willed yourself to where you are now, be that for better or worse. Now you are ready to proceed to the next part of this guide.

10

Cosmic Time

Time, as we know it, is manmade. Sometimes it is difficult to separate myth from fact, but even so, here I want to show you how time may have some bearing on a 'new age' that could be dawning.

Over the years, as industry and inventions have taken us forward, mankind has become less and less influenced by religion, and more and more influenced by science.

In order to reveal certain matters I go back to the 7th century Mayan prophet Pacal Votan (603 – 683 A.D.). He left a chilling universal message for future generations of an evolving Earth. Pacal claimed that if humanity wanted to save itself from 'biospheric destruction' then we must 'return to living in natural time.' Certainly I do not want to begin an argument about saving the earth from destruction, but I need to show you what is possible because of the past.

Before I can reveal what could be in the future, I feel it worthy to give you some details relating to Pacal Votan. You do not need to study what I write of this man, but let the facts speak for themselves. Pacal Votan, known as a magician of time, ruled the empire of Nah Chan Palenque (in present day Chiapas, Mexico). His understanding of mathematics was way ahead of his time.

His claims that 'God is a number' and 'God is in all' are, perhaps, the keys to unlocking an age-old question, 'Where is God?' Which goes back to the belief of some, that God is in the head - a manmade deity.

Ahead of his time, Pacal knew that humanity, as a species, would become disconnected from the laws of the natural world and would lose touch with nature. He also knew that modern humanity would be put to the test to see if we could regain our conscious connection to natural time, evolving beyond the constructs of manmade linear time.

'What does this all have to do with cosmic connections?', some of you may well ask. Well, let's take the date of 21 December, 2012. As prophesised by Pacal, the date in question is said to bring regeneration of the Earth, offering awakening to all open, willing hearts. Had it just been the prophecy of Pacal that claimed this, then it might have fallen on deaf ears. But many peoples spoke of these last days of the 'Great Cycle': the Maya, Hopi, Egyptians, Kabbalists, Essenes, Qero elders of Peru, Navajo, Cherokee, Apache, Iroquois confederacy, Dogon Tribe, and Aborigines.

Now is not the time to go into mathematical equations as to how this particular date of 2012 came about being prophesised, as I want to get on to channelling your energies in targeting what you desire. Pacal Votan also taught his Mayan people (approx 435 A.D. - 830 A.D.) the handling of the 7 powers held in the human body.

He used to point out the parts of his initiates' bodies where that great power, coming from the cosmos, would flow out. It has been said that even after finishing

104

his physical life, the teacher Pacal Votan continued travelling in other dimensions spreading this wisdom.

Using a true story, I want to show you what I mean by a 'cosmic connection'. For the Mayans, the dead became stars, and when children were born these stars came down and became their souls.

Along Pacal Votan's coffin lid there are many Mayan glyphs representing the other planets, because they also believed that souls could come from another planet of our solar system, and that the souls of the most evolved children may have come from even the most distant celestial bodies or stars.

The pyramid that housed Pacal's body is unquestionably the most extraordinary structure ever built by an American people before the arrival of white men. The coffin that holds his body, in the mortuary chamber of the Temple of the Inscriptions, is big and sumptuous.

One of its features is something that is described as a 'psycho-duct'. This was considered to be a magic conduit, and comes out from the coffin in the shape of a snake made of lime and white stones. This magic conduit was set up so that Pacal Votan could communicate permanently with his people, and his messages could always be heard through the priests. It was also used by the priests to communicate with this deified being, to ask for his advice.

In order for the Mayan priests to communicate with Pacal Votan, they had to reach a very deep meditative state; only then could true communication take place. Amazing as it may seem, the first thing that the priests would hear was a sound indicating the presence of Pacal Votan. Even more amazing is that when the tomb was opened in 1952, they found 9 metal sheet-shaped white stones, which produced a metallic sound when they collided against each other. This was the sound the priests would have heard.

Just as the priests made contact with Pacal, you will be able to communicate your desires to the cosmos through your own 'magic conduit'. You will have an amazing experience, and be able to go on to better things.

The Maya are known as Supreme Masters of Time Magic. They are perhaps best known for recording an unsurpassed system of planetary and galactic time cycles, and they believed that the Milky Way Galaxy was the generator of life. The architect of the universe was known by many names, such as The One Giver of Movement and Measure; The Absolute Being; The Centre of the Galaxy; and The Universal Dynamism. It is that which stimulates and motivates life in its total manifestation of spirit and matter; the principle of intelligent energy that pervades the entire universe, animate or inanimate.

Mayan science was not separate from their religion; their universal philosophy was that the human body belongs to the earth, and the human spirit to the Universe. The Maya understood human existence as nothing less than a faithful reflection of cosmic energy.

As manifestations of cosmic consciousness, the Maya regarded all things and beings that exist on Earth as products of the projection of energy in the form of vibration. Their world-view is a paradigm based on wave harmonics and resonant fields. The Mayan sages were aware of the sensory and extrasensory characteristics of trees and plants, and, understanding that the tree is the best regenerator of the air we breathe, revered it.

The Maya did not have a mythical concept of deities, but instead maintained that lords represented the forces of nature. As pioneers of the mathematical concept of zero, they depicted zero in the form of an eye because it has great spiritual implications and represents the essence of the beginning, the seed from which all life springs, the Great Mystery.

It is documented that the Classic Maya trained and sensitised their physical, astral, and mental bodies to such a degree that they became human 'observatories.' That is the dedication and belief they had in themselves, just as you too will dedicate your thoughts to what you want, and will come to believe in yourself.

It is difficult to account for how the Maya knew of 400 stars in the 7 Sisters constellation called the Pleiades, whereas today we can only spot 6 with the naked eye. Thanks to three generations of scholars, we now have access to some of the primary codes constituting their cosmic knowledge. The calendar cycles of the Maya are highly relevant to us in this day and age because all of their stone records point to an end-point synchronization of AD 21 December, 2012.

You have to wonder why the Maya people, so long ago, laboured so greatly to carve huge stone markers alerting us of this date. They believed that this date would be the end of our Earth's current 26,000 year evolutionary cycle. Perhaps it was a wake-up call to those of us here in the present day, telling us to mend our ways. Perhaps it was to awaken the urgent need to return to living in harmony with the laws of nature, and to make us conscious of the critical, transformative powers now enveloping the planet.

The Maya developed mathematics based on a system of 20 (20 fingers and toes), and with this were able to make astronomical and temporal calculations of fantastic levels. In some of the Mayan sites we have what appear to be dates that go back 400 million years, or even 25 billion years. The Maya used more than 17 calendars; no other contemporaneous people on Earth even came close to their sophistication in this regard. They computed the length of the Earth's revolution around the Sun to within a thousandth of a decimal point of the calculations of modern science, without the use of our precision instruments. Not only that, but they kept calendars of the lunar and eclipse cycles, equinox and solstices, and even maintained calendars recording synodical revolutions, and synchronisations of the revolutions of Mercury, Venus, Mars, Jupiter and Saturn.

The suspicion dawns that the calendar is more than a calendar. The number system, so exquisitely proportioned, is also a means for recording harmonic calibrations. These relate not just to space-time positioning, but to resonant qualities of being and experience, whose nature our materialistic predisposition blinds us to.

And this is where I was leading. The Mayans, it seems, wanted to place the Earth and its solar system in synchronisation within a larger galactic community. Our minds have become dulled with the passage of time; the smog of modernisation has stifled our senses and our spirits have become weakened by lazy living. I hope this story has given you the impetus to search within you, within the creative parts of your mind, for the pieces that fit together to make you spiritually whole again. If the dawning of a New Era is upon us, then let us make it work to our advantage.

11

Super Fast Track Your Cosmic Order

It has been suggested that man cannot become one with the universe, that it is impossible. I am not going to argue about this, as I am not preaching to the cynics. You have faith in yourself, and in time you will come to make your own cosmic connection. I will leave it for you to decide if you became one with the universe.

In an earlier chapter I showed you how to convey your desires to the cosmos, but here I am going to show you a way to fast track your order. You will have a direct link and, therefore, will have a chance to secure things more rapidly than you would have believed possible. There is no secret to what you will soon be doing.

Ordering

Please read through what follows in this chapter and familiarise yourself with the guidelines. Even do a practice run a few times, if you wish. Remember, do not try too hard. The point of this method is to become as relaxed as possible. One word of warning: it is not worthwhile doing this when you are fatigued, as you may just fall asleep. Mentally suggest to yourself that you will remember all that occurs during the upcoming session, and that it will be beneficial to your well-being.

Step 1 – *Find a quiet thinking place*
This could be any place you find comfortable. You might have dropped a friend off somewhere, and they have asked if you can wait for them. Lock the car doors and take advantage of the spare time. Please do not try this in any place where you could be vulnerable to harm or attack from strangers, e.g. public places. Even the garden shed can be a place of cosmic peace. A strong word of warning: if you live near an electricity sub-station, pylon, or any large electrical installation, you may be better off going someplace away from these interferences.

Step 2 – *Relax*
Relaxing and winding down are not things we are all accustomed to doing. Our modern world is full of fast-living gadgetry, and time-saving devices. Relaxing goes against all that has been instilled in us. Learn to sit down and relax in surroundings that are comfortable. Remove any jewellery that may irritate you, and draw the curtains or close the blinds. Just let yourself go, close your eyes.

Step 3 – *Become one with yourself*
Becoming one with yourself means to become attuned to your inner self. Please make yourself comfortable. Sit down or lie down. Adjust your clothing . . . footwear . . . eyeglasses.

- Quiet your mind . . .
- Still your thoughts . . .
- Relax your body . . .
- Feel your face . . . your jaw . . . relaxing . . .
- Feel your shoulders . . . your neck . . . relaxing
- Your arms . . . your hands . . . feel at peace . . .

- Your torso . . . your hips . . . letting go . . .
- Your legs . . . your feet . . . totally relaxed . . .
- Focus on your breathing.
- Inhale slowly and deeply through your nose . . .
- Retain the breath as long as is comfortable . . .
- Exhale through the mouth slowly and completely . . .
- Repeat (inhale 1, exhale 2, inhale 3 . . . until you are comfortable)

Step 4 – *Influence yourself to relax even more*
The phone should be unplugged (don't forget to plug it back in afterwards!). Play some soothing music; ensure that the room temperature is neither too hot, nor too cold. Refrain from drinking stimulants prior to this. Make sure that others are aware of your relaxation period. Use the toilet beforehand if need be.

Step 5 – *Visualise what you want, see yourself doing it*
Imagery is a powerful tool. Prior to this you should have been using such a tool to prepare what you will be focusing on at this stage. Perhaps, as an example, if you are good at, or enjoy watching football, you will imagine yourself kicking a ball at the cosmos, each ball loaded with a request. You can do this with almost anything you want. Imagine yourself in a great big garden, for you gardeners. Each seed you plant, or new plant you put in the soil, is a request. Have a quick practice run, so you get the hang of it.

Step 6 – *Be absolutely positive beyond belief*
At this stage you should have unwavering belief in what you are doing, and an air of expectancy.

Step 7 – *Eradicate negative thoughts*
Eradicate negative thoughts from your mind; each negative thought is a thieving hand come to steal your requests. Counter the thief by sending an imaginary policeman to arrest it. Remember how we turned negatives into positives; use that tool to rid yourself of doubt. Doubtful thoughts can come back to haunt you.

Step 8 – *Refocus your thoughts*
Having trouble refocusing? Get quiet. Stop what you are doing, and just sit or lie down for 5 minutes. Close your eyes to eliminate visual stimuli. If your thoughts are still racing, focus on your breathing. When your thoughts have calmed down, redirect them to the positive thought or feeling you want to focus on. Take a minute or two to immerse yourself in it before you go on.

Step 9 – *Cosmic Connection*
Now you are ready to start connecting. In order to stimulate the magnetic field around the pineal gland (cosmic eye), allow your mind to focus on the midway point between the pineal gland and the pituitary body (remember where I said they were). The creative part of your mind will start to function without any effort. With your eyes closed, you should be concentrating on the pineal gland. This is achieved by staring at a point in the middle of the forehead. Do not force yourself to do this, and do not strain the muscles of the eye. Just think of doing it and it will happen automatically. Your cosmic eye will become activated, maybe only a little at first, but with regular application of this method it will awaken even more.

Beginning with withdrawal of the senses and physical consciousness, higher consciousness is in the region of the pineal gland. The perceptive faculty and the point of realisation are centralised in the area between the middle of the forehead and the pineal gland. The trick is to visualise, very intently, the subtle body escaping through the trap door of the brain. A popping sound may occur at the time of separation of the astral body in the area of the pineal gland, so do not be alarmed if it feels like that is happening.

Time and space have no meaning, just as your conscious thoughts are meaningless. Allow your requests to be directed at the cosmos. In this state you can do anything – run a mile in a second, climb Mount Everest naked, anything – all from the comfort of wherever you are relaxing.

You will be in a place where hours can seem like seconds, there is no sense of time or urgency. Your mind can be free of all earthly constraints. You can speak without talking, channel your spiritual energy to wherever you want it to go. Ask of the cosmos what you desire, and see it happening without fear of failure. Before long you will be able to carry out this practice at will, even dispensing with my suggestions and creating your own ideas for a connection.

12

Accelerated Cosmic Connection

As a certified clinical hypnotherapist I have placed many clients in a hypnotic state. During a session clients can bring messages from:

- other aspects of themselves
- other dimensions of reality
- their unconscious mind
- another entity

However, in this case, you will be fine-tuning your self-hypnosis skills in order to make a deeper cosmic connection. Most certainly, the method you used in the preceding chapter will have connected you to the cosmos, have no worries about that. This method will allow you a different way to connect besides activating your cosmic eye. There are advantages to using self-hypnosis to induce a state of connection, and these are:

- allows for a smoother transition and thus avoids the 'bang' affect
- allows you to remain in the linear time to which you are accustomed

- speeds up the function of the cosmic eye without conscious effort
- makes better use of your subconscious under a controlled situation
- stimulates other areas of brain function

You will be in control of yourself throughout self-induced hypnosis, have no fear about that. The stage hypnotists you see on TV, or in pubs and clubs, only use people who would normally do outrageous things. I could do such tricks, but my code of ethics makes me a far better person than to try to turn people into laughing stocks. You will not turn yourself into one of those people using this method. This is a clinical matter, not a matter for theatrics.

Already, today, whilst you have gone about your everyday duties, you would have slipped into trance at least half a dozen times, without even noticing it. All you are going to do now is to slip into such a trance at will, as opposed to how you usually do it throughout the day. Have you ever noticed that when talking to a friend, they may not have been listening to a word you said, although they were looking right at you? Perhaps something that you said early on triggered them to go into trance. Even just looking at something (fascination) can send you off into trance; that is how easy it is to slip into. Ask someone for directions and they go into a trance-like state; watch them look up into their brain. You have just put someone into a trance.

Then there is the person who totally denies ever having been in trance, and who defies any effort to go into trance, through fear of looking silly. Well, too late, they have already been in trance. This is not to be perceived as a battle of wills. In fact, the more intelligent a person is, the easier it is for them to slip off into trance.

There are no prizes for defying yourself, as it will be you who is putting yourself into trance. If you were able to accomplish what was in the preceding chapter then this will be just as easy. There is no compunction for you to carry this out, if you feel uncomfortable with the idea of it. It is best to stick with whatever suits you, but this method will allow for a far better connection. This guide is not about curative hypnotherapy, so please do not use what I am going to teach you as an aid for anything but connecting to the cosmos. Leave the curing to the professionals.

Hypnotherapy goes past the conscious mind and taps into the emotional body - the inner child - the place where we store issues that we have to deal with, but are not yet ready to. To heal physically, one must heal the emotional aspect of the issue first or it will resurface in another way. So, please, stick to what I am going to explain to you. There is no need to learn anything else, not unless you are fascinated by the subject and want to take it further as a profession, or for self-help.

I do have one piece of advice though. Please remember that not everyone is a candidate for hypnotherapy. When doing hypnosis it is necessary to use the brain's natural ability to produce a deeply relaxed state. Hypnosis occurs primarily in the alpha and theta states, but can occur during any of the brainwave patterns.

- Beta – this is the fastest of the brain waves. It is the waking state.

- Alpha – this is a restful, relaxing state. Hypnosis induces this state.
- Theta – this is a deep state of relaxation. Deep hypnosis occurs at this state.
- Delta – this is the sleeping state.

It is a deeper state of mental relaxation than meditation, in which the person is aware of their surroundings. Hypnotherapy can also be used to explore past/parallel lives, during which time blockages created in other lifetimes can be viewed and released.

Before commencing the self-induced hypnosis session there are a few things to cover. The idea of the session is to allow you to explore a different method of connecting to the cosmos. With this method there is no baggage: you get there, do your business and leave. Remember, the hypnotic state is something you go into at least half a dozen times a day, even more for children. Put your thumb a few millimetres from the end of your nose. Stare at it and feel yourself drifting off. That is how easy it is.

When in the hypnotic state, you will still be aware of what is going on around you. For instance, if someone knocked on your door, then you would safely awaken, as you would not be in a sleeping state. At no time would you lose your grip on reality, although if you are fatigued you may fall asleep, and then you would not hear a knock on the door. It is best to avoid going into trance when fatigued, as you can then wake up feeling grumpy.

Immediately after you come out of trance, remain where you are for a few minutes. Gather your thoughts until the trance is fully over. Perhaps you would like to look at some of the suggested scripts you could use in the following chapter when in a state of trance. You say them in your head when in trance. Remember, it helps to pre-plan your session.

Self-induced accelerated cosmic connection

Step 1 – *Find a quiet place*
Again, as before, this could be any place you find comfortable, but not somewhere public where you might be vulnerable.

Step 2 – *Surroundings*
As in the previous chapter, learn to sit down and relax in surroundings that are comfortable. Remove any jewellery that may irritate you, and draw the curtains, or close the blinds. Just let yourself go, close your eyes.

Step 3 – *Become one with yourself*
Becoming one with yourself means to become attuned to your inner self. Please make yourself comfortable. Sit down or lie down. Adjust your clothing so that nothing intrudes on your meditation.

Step 4 – *Breathing*
Focus on your breathing:

- Inhale slowly and deeply through your nose . . .
- Retain the breath as long as is comfortable . . .
- Exhale through the mouth slowly and completely . . .
- Repeat for two more breaths, or until you are comfortable

Step 5 – *Relax your body (should take about two or three minutes)*
If you choose to use them, there are some very good relaxation CDs available from accredited suppliers.

- Start with your face . . . let your jaw drop . . . relaxing
- Feel your shoulders sinking . . . your neck . . . relaxing
- Let your arms go . . . your hands . . . feel at peace . . .
- Your torso . . . your hips . . . letting go . . .
- Your legs . . . your feet . . . your toes ... totally relaxed . . .

Give yourself the mental suggestion that you will remember all that occurs during the upcoming session that will be beneficial to your well-being.

Step 6 – *Induction technique*
This is just one of about 100 or so different induction methods. There are some very good self-hypnosis audio-CDs available from accredited suppliers. Remember, hypnosis is not sleep. You can sit in a comfortable chair, but even whilst lying on the bed or couch you can perform this technique.

- Pick an imaginary spot above your head, and without moving your head, look up with your eyes, through your eyebrows.
- Keep you eyes focused on this imaginary spot, but do not overly strain your eye muscles.
- As your eyes are focused, say to yourself (in your mind): 'I'm going to count down from 5. With each and every count, my eyelids will become heavier.'

- '5 ... So sleepy...' (emphasise the 's' sound), 'so tired'.
- '4 ... My eyelids becoming heavier and heavier, so sleepy, so tired'.
- '3 ... My eyelids beginning to close all by themselves, they are so tired'.
- '2 ... And now my eyelids closing, closing, closing, closing, closing, closing, closing, closing, closing them, close them, so sleepy, so tired'.
- '1 ...' (Your eyes should now be closed, but you should still be aware that you are *not* asleep).

Step 7 – *Deepener*
Take yourself down to a deeper state of hypnosis, where the subconscious part of your mind starts to take control of the cosmic connection. With your eyes closed and following on from step 6, say (in your mind) the following, slowly:

> 'I am just like a leaf, falling gently from a tree, sinking, deeper and deeper. As I count down from five, with each and every count I am sinking deeper and deeper. I am sinking' (again, emphasising the 's' sound), 'floating down, deeper and deeper. 5 – Slowly sinking further and further down. 4 ...'

Do this until you are down to number '1'. You should now be in a deep state of hypnosis, and your subconscious will be in control. Just for security's sake, add the words, 'Should the need arise, I will come out of trance for safety's sake.' This way you are always giving yourself an embedded command to follow your senses.

Step 8 – *Cosmic Connection*
While in this state, just talk in your mind. Talk about what is going to happen. Using words along the lines of: 'My cosmic eye is speaking to the universe. I want that connection to be made with ease.' After this opening monologue you can enhance on what it is you want, or want to do or become; whatever it is you desire. Images usually work best. Remember when you imagined that cup a few chapters ago? Visualise your desires. See whatever it is you want happening to you.

In this state you are aware of everything, and yet, strangely, you are not aware. Your subconscious mind is listening to you; your conscious mind is not listening. Although your conscious mind is sleeping, you will still be able to awaken if the need should arise. What goes on here need not awaken your conscious mind, which does not mind taking a backseat to your subconscious thoughts.

Step 9 – *Coming out of the cosmic connection*
Once you have finished requesting your desires and want to terminate your cosmic connection, you should say in your mind:

> 'After the count of 1 I will awaken and feel completely refreshed.
> 3. I'm beginning to awaken.
> 2. I'm coming out of it.
> 1. Awaken, my eyes opening slowly.'

You will now be fully awake. Stay where you are for a few minutes before getting up.

In time you will be able to master this technique with ease. You will know when you have mastered it, and then you can really make some inroads into making your dreams become reality. In time you will try different techniques that you pick up, until you have a tailor-made method that you feel comfortable with.

Remember, the unconscious part of your mind always believes what you are telling it whilst you are in this state of mind, and you can use the time to give yourself some positive suggestions or affirmations. Good luck.

13

Cosmic Scripts

You do not need to memorise the following scripts word for word, they are just general guides to assist you. In fact, you can purchase such scripts, there are hundreds available. No matter how you wish to convey your desires to the cosmos, there is a script for just about every single situation. In time, you will be able to devise your own scripts, even adlib them as you go along. Even if you do not want to use self-induced hypnosis to make the cosmic connection, these scripts can still be used to convey what you want. Should you be tackling a personal problem via your cosmic connection, then spend that session just on that one problem. Work on one goal at a time.

Always be positive within your script, and reinforce what you want by positive use of your words. Don't say, 'I don't want to be fat.' Instead say, 'With every day that passes I am becoming slimmer and more attractive looking to those around me.' Don't say, 'I haven't got a decent carpet.' Instead say, 'I can see the carpet I am going to get, it is ...'

Be careful what you ask for. Asking for better health, without saying that you are already healthy, could lead to an unexpected visit to the hospital. Sometimes 'better' health needs surgery to get rid of 'bad' health, if you follow my meaning. Always start by saying that your health is good, and you want to see it remain so. If you are poorly, you can go along the lines of, 'I have endured bad health for many years, and as every day passes I am becoming healthier by natural means. My body is helping to repair itself.'

You might ask for a new house, but you may end up with a doll's house! Carefully phrase your requests. Be specific. I once asked for a house to be sold, and I named the street. Two houses in that particular named street sold within a week, but not the one I wanted sold. Name the place, the number, etc.

This is a rich universe; there is plenty for us all. Your request to the cosmos is not an affirmation; you are not just saying these things to yourself. Do not mix up affirmations with your cosmic connection; here you are telling the cosmos what you want.

Remember, always accentuate the positive and make it as unambiguous as possible. The scripts below are not tailor-made for you, although you can have them tailored to your exact needs by specialists. Try writing your own script, using those below as examples. When you have finished writing your own scripts, store them to memory. They can act as a means of communicating your needs to the cosmos, so you will be giving yourself every possible chance of manifesting what you desire.

Self-improvement script

Cosmos, I am learning all of the time, and I know I will learn more and more about *(insert what you want to learn about)*. I lead a good life and I want it to continue, becoming even better than it is now. Always help me learn more and guide me to things that are for my

128

betterment. I am a good person, I want to be an even a better person. I am understanding of others, give me an even better understanding of those around me. I am able to grasp complicated ideas, and as each day passes I will be able to grasp even more. I want you, as appropriate, to make my life run smoothly, and to make these things happen from this moment onwards. I want to continue to improve as time goes on. Thank you for listening, I leave you with this in peace.

Confidence script

Cosmos, I am learning to become comfortable and confident when speaking to other people, help me become even more comfortable and relaxed. I can express myself, and I know that you can help me to improve, and express myself more clearly and confidently. I have a sense of humour, and I know you will make that sense of humour be seen by people, when appropriate. I look forward to speaking with people, and I can improve on this. I want you, as appropriate, to make my life run smoothly and to make these things happen from this moment onwards. I want to continue to improve as time goes on. Thank you for listening, I leave you with this in peace.

Better job, pay, or status script

Cosmos, I have a lot to offer a new employer. My skills are worth securing and I am a hard worker. I could not fail to impress any new or potential employer. As soon as I have that new job I will impress the new boss, as I have the ability to do good work. With your help I will be giving someone a great opportunity when they employ me. I do my job very well; I work hard and deserve to be paid a higher wage. All my needs, desires and goals are met instantaneously because I am one with the universe. A higher wage will give me even more things than I have now. I have worked in the community of mankind and during the course of my work I have become a better person, my status in life will now improve. I know I will get a higher wage. I want you, as appropriate, to make my life run smoothly and to make these things happen from this moment onwards. I want to continue to improve as time goes on. Thank you for listening, I leave you with this in peace.

Chemotherapy treatment script

Cosmos, my chemotherapy treatment is designed to make me better. My health is returning, as is my strength. I am better able to handle my chemotherapy sessions and know that you can make me handle them with more ease, as time goes on. With your help I will handle these treatments in deep peace. My hair will grow back and become as strong as ever, and my sickness will shrink. With your help it will become more tolerable and I will regain even more of my vitality. I want you, as appropriate, to make my life run smoothly and to make these things happen from this moment onwards. I want to continue to improve as time goes on. Thank you for listening, I leave you with this in peace.

New or improved relationships script

Cosmos, I am a warm, loving person with a lot to offer. I have the ability to listen to the needs of others. Allowing this side of me to be seen will attract people to me, especially those people I want to attract. I have desire in my eyes, and I know that I can use it any time I want to. I have love in my heart, and can give this love to the one I know will love me back. I want you, as appropriate, to make my life run smoothly and to make these things happen from this moment onwards. I want to continue to improve as time goes on. Thank you for listening, I leave you with this in peace.

Weight loss script

Cosmos, my metabolism works to burn calories; I know it can become even faster than it already is. My metabolism is going to increase, as appropriate, and burn more calories. I drink water during the course of the day; I know that by drinking more water I will drop excess weight, and cellulite. I love food, and now I will distinguish what is good for me, only eating the things that are nutritious and healthy. I have no need to eat stodgy food; my body is too valuable to abuse with such foodstuffs. I have great willpower, and I ask you to make my willpower even stronger, as appropriate. I want you, as appropriate, to make my life run smoothly and to make these things happen from this moment onwards. I want to continue to improve as time goes on. Thank you for listening, I leave you with this in peace.

Wealth script

Cosmos, already I am wealthy in knowledge and am able to survive on the money I make. I know that I will never starve, or fail to be looked after, if the need for that arose. My earning power is incredible and strong. I have the ability to make a lot more money, and to achieve great success. I know that with your help my cash income will rise dramatically. I am, and will always be, in the right place at the right time. This is a rich universe and there is plenty for all of us. I am industrious and prepared to work to make this happen. The right opportunity will come along, and with your help it will happen very soon. I know I will have good fortune every moment of my life. I am open to receive the cash in abundance that the universe has for me, and ask that this will manifest in my life right now. I will become a magnet for wealth. My life is going to change for the better. I have great willpower, and I ask you to make my willpower even stronger. I want you, as appropriate, to make my life run smoothly and to make these things happen from this moment onwards. I want to continue to improve as time goes on. Thank you for listening, I leave you with this in peace.

Have you ever heard of the self-fulfilling prophecy syndrome? This is a prediction that, in being made, actually causes itself to come true. I fell into that phase – I predicted that everything I ever laid my hands on would turn to mush, and it did. My negative expectations were always fulfilled. I do not intend to give a clumsy scenario, I am sure you all get what I mean. We have, almost certainly, all heard someone say, 'One day so-and-so is going to get their comeuppance.' The prophecy is then set in motion, and all you can do is wait for it to happen. Take my advice, only think and speak in positive ways. Remember, lucky people think and behave in ways that create good fortune in their lives. When planning what you are going to ask of the cosmos, use some of these positive phrases:

- I am open to receive the abundant good that the universe has for me.

- Everything good is coming to me easily and effortlessly.
- This is a rich universe and there is plenty for all of us.
- My highest good is manifesting in my life right now.
- I always get everything that is for my highest good.
- I envision only that which is for my highest good.
- Wealth flows to me in avalanches of abundance.
- I expect good fortune every moment of my life.
- I am always in the right place at the right time.
- I expect life to give me what is best for me.
- I deserve the best and it comes to me now.
- I now eagerly await my greatest good.
- Cosmos is the source of all my good.
- I am cosmically guided in all I do.
- I expect the best and I get it now.

Focus more on your desires than on your doubts, and the dream will take care of itself. You may be surprised at how easily this happens. Your doubts are not as powerful as your desires, unless you make them so. Remember, think wealthy and you become wealthy. Why try to predict the future? Make it happen.

14

Cosmic Sense

The ability to connect to the universe has some amazing perks; one of them is the awakening of the 'sixth sense'. Traditionally humans have been thought to come equipped with five senses: sight, hearing, taste, touch, and smell. Animals possess several extra senses, including altered vision and hearing, echolocation, electric and/or magnetic field detection, and supplementary chemical detection senses.

In addition to taste and smell, most vertebrates use Jacobson's organ (a chemosensory organ located in the nasal septum, or roof of the mouth, in vertebrates. It is also known as: Vomeronasal Organ, Vomeronasal Pits.). It is used to detect trace quantities of chemicals. This system has its own separate organs, nerves, and connecting structures in the brain. The function of the vomeronasal system is the detection of pheromones, chemical messengers that carry information between individuals of the same species.

It was widely believed that humans had long ago discarded this sensory system somewhere along evolution's trail. But convincing behavioural and anatomical evidence has since brought the notion of a human vomeronasal organ (VNO) into the realm of scientific fact.

In the 1800s, Danish physician Ludwig Jacobson detected structures in a patient's nose that became termed 'Jacobson's organ' (although the organ was actually first reported in humans by F Ruysch in 1703). Since its discovery, comparisons of human and animal embryos led scientists to conclude that Jacobson's organ in humans corresponded to the pits in snakes and vomeronasal organs in other mammals, but the organ was thought to be vestigial (no longer functional) in humans.

While humans don't display the Flehmen reaction (when your cat smells something, opens his mouth slightly, then wrinkles his nose and curls back his upper lip), recent studies have demonstrated that Jacobson's organ functions as in other mammals to detect pheromones and to sample low concentrations of certain non-human chemicals in air. There are indications that Jacobson'' organ may be stimulated in pregnant women, perhaps partially accounting for an improved sense of smell during pregnancy and possibly implicated in morning sickness.

Since extra-sensory perception (ESP) is awareness of the world beyond the senses, it would be inappropriate to term this Sixth Sense 'extrasensory'. After all, the vomeronasal organ connects to the amygdala of the brain and relays information about the surroundings in essentially the same manner as any other sense. Like ESP, however, the sixth sense remains somewhat elusive and hard to describe.

Since the dawn of thought, it has been the dream of the spiritually aspiring to achieve that supreme state of mind that only the most legendary figures have come to experience. Men and woman of science have kept this dream alive for centuries, exploring the visual, kinaesthetic and auditory pathways of the human body, in a relentless pursuit for the *ultimate solution.*

Finally the time has come. You now have the knowledge and understanding to create a powerfully effective and easy-to-wield method of channelling the mind into its optimal state. At will, you will be able to produce the brainwave patterns of those astonishing individuals who lead rather than follow, and win rather than waver.

After the Asian tsunami, scientists struggled to explain reports that primitive aboriginal tribesmen had somehow sensed the impending danger in time to join wild animals in a life-saving flight to higher ground. A new theory suggests that the anterior cingulate cortex, described by some scientists as part of the brain's 'oops' center (the part of the brain that alerts a person to the fact they have made a mistake), may actually function as an early warning system - one that works at a subconscious level to help us recognise and avoid high-risk situations.

While some scientists discount the existence of a sixth sense for danger, new research from Washington University in St Louis has identified a brain region that clearly acts as an early warning system – one that monitors environmental cues, weighs possible consequences and helps us adjust our behavior to avoid dangerous situations. This sixth sense is something that develops within you as time goes on.

'Our brains are better at picking up subtle warning signs than we previously thought,' said Joshua Brown, Ph.D., a research associate in psychology, and co-author of a study on these findings published in the journal *Science*. The findings offer rigorous scientific evidence for a new way of conceptualising the complex executive control processes taking place in and around the anterior cingulate cortex (ACC), a brain area located near the top of the frontal lobes and along the walls that divide the left and right hemispheres.

Although we all possess a sixth sense, many neglect to heed what it is telling them. How many times have you made a mistake and then realised you already knew of it before it happened? This brain region can actually learn to recognise when you might make a mistake, even before you have made it. This early warning system can be of great benefit if you allow it to work. By heeding your sixth sense you can be warned in advance when your behavior might lead to a negative outcome, so that you can avoid making such a mistake.

For a long time I have been interested in how the brain integrates cognitive information about the world with our emotions, and how we come to feel about things the way that we do. When I developed my own sixth sense, I was better able to grasp how I was able to listen to it.

For many reasons, people think the ACC might be the brain structure responsible for merging these different signals. It seems to be an area that's involved in deciding what information gets prioritised in the decision-making process. It seems able to link motivationalñe and effect information – like the concepts of goodness or badness – and to use this information to bring about changes in cognition, to alter how we think about things. Once you start to connect to the universe you will feel the benefits of this dormant sixth sense.

While more and more people agree that the cingulate plays an important role in complex thoughts and feelings, there are competing theories regarding the cognitive mechanisms that underlie activity there.

The ACC is better understood as a pre-emptive early warning system, one that is actively working to help us anticipate the potential for mistakes, and thus avoid them altogether.

The ACC has been the focus of intensive scientific research in recente years because it plays a critical role in the brain's processing of especially complex and challenging cognitive tasks. Abnormalities in the region are closely associated with a host of serious mental problems, including schizophrenia and obsessive-compulsive disorder.

To test this hypothesis, an experiment was conducted requiring healthy young people to respond to a series of cues on a computer screen. Participants were presented with either a white or a blue dash, which soon changed into a small arrow pointing either right or left. They were instructed to quickly push one of two buttons depending on the arrow's direction. To simulate conflict, researchers occasionally slipped in a larger second arrow that required participants to change gears and push the opposite button.

The idea is that at some point you have these competing tendencies – to push the right or left button – and both are active in the brain at the same time, which creates conflict. Some theories suggest that whenever you see these two arrows, this state of conflict is engaged, and it's the state of conflict that is being detected by the cingulate.

By increasing the delay before presentation of the larger second arrow, researchers raised the odds that an individual would reach 'the point of no return' and thus be unable to change gears in time to avoid pushing the wrong button. They then adjusted the delay time over many trials so that each participant eventually exhibited error rates of about 50 per cent when provided with an initial blue priming dash, compared with error rates of only 4 percent when presented with a white priming dash.

Using functional magnetic resonance imaging (fMRI), researchers captured images of brain activity at 2.5-second intervals throughout the experiment. One of the resarchers said, 'We didn't tell them that the white or blue cue offered any clue about their likelihood of making an error on any particular trial, but by the end of the session, some of them had begun to figure it out, at least on a subconscious level.'

Even among those who remained consciously unaware of the blue cue's significance, researchers found that simply showing the blue colour was eventually enough to spark increased activity in the cingulate, and that this effect strengthened over time as the subject became more familiar with the task. Brain imaging suggested that an area of the brain had learned to recognise that blue cues indicated a greater potential for error, thus providing an early warning signal that negative consequences were likely to follow their behavior.

Thus, brain imaging confirmed that the ACC had 'learned' the significance of the blue cue, and had begun, at least subconsciously, to adjust behaviors accordingly, the study found.

By providing a clearer picture of the cognitive mechanisms by which we self-monitor and control our behaviour, the study is an important step in efforts to develop more effective treatments for mental illness. It also provides a new way of understanding inappropriate behaviors that often accompany mental illnesses.

The results suggest how impairment of the ACC mechanisms in schizophrenia can lead to breakdowns in the early warning system, so that the brain fails to pre-empt or control inappropriate behavior. In individuals with obsessive-compulsive disorder, the ACC might warn of an impending problem even when no problem is imminent. What I am getting at here is that it appears that this area of the brain is somehow figuring things out without us having to be consciously aware of it, just like when I asked you to read some of the chapters of this book without applying any conscious effort.

This mechanism exists because there are plenty of situations in our everyday lives that require the brain to monitor subtle changes in our environment and adjust our behavior, even in cases where we may not be necessarily aware of the conditions that prompted the adjustment. In some cases, the brain's ability to monitor subtle environmental changes and make adjustments may actually be even more robust if it takes place on a subconscious level. This is the case when you connect to the universe. Your brain works on a subconscious level, without any effort being applied. All that you have to do is take heed of your newfound sixth sense.

The researchers also tested their theory using another computer model that had been previously developed to support an existing theory of the ACC as a system focused on conflict resolution. By simulating both models they could then adjudicate between them and do so in a way where they forced each one to make predictions that they only tested after the fact.

Everyone is aware of his or her five basic senses: seeing, feeling, smelling, hearing and tasting. What everyone is not so well aware of is their sixth sense; that sense of otherworldliness, a connection to something more and greater than their physical senses are able to perceive. This is the entrance to the world of the unseen encounter, the unheard communication, the unfelt touch of someone from the spiritual world trying to make a connection with someone in the physical body.

The sixth sense is a part of everyone whether or not they like it. It is a normal part of the human psyche and not reserved for special or gifted persons. Thanks to the media and to religion it has been misrepresented, and as a result, people regard the spirit world with fear and trepidation. A person has more to fear going to their car in the parking lot after work than from those souls in the spirit world. Contrary to what we might see in movies, or read about in books, I have never seen a newspaper headline where those in spirit, without physical bodies, carried out evil deeds like a mugger in a parking lot. But I do not want to go too deeply into the subject matter of what some call the spirit world. I will leave that for another book I am working on, which will be called something along the lines of *Cosmic Ordering Your Afterlife*.

Every human being is equipped from birth with what they need to communicate with the spirit world. This is the same scientific phenomenon that works in the transmission of electronic information such as the television or radio. It is also no different than using electromagnetic energy to connect to the cosmos. These connections are like tuning into a particular band or frequency to get the program that you want. The sixth sense is similar in that it requires tuning in to the frequency that allows a connection.

I am amazed at the mumbo-jumbo some of these spiritualists come out with. I remember when I was researching a book for a victim of crime; I had to visit some spiritualist churches. Some of the spiritualists were making connections, but some looked to be faking it. However, I do not want to knock something that, in the right hands, can be of great comfort to the bereaved.

I wonder what would happen if spiritualists expressed their connection as electrical rather than psychic? Would there still be as many people who are convinced that it is a sham if it was expressed in terminology that they were familiar with? Electronic tuning is done through electronic means that is mechanical in nature. Spiritual tuning is done through the brain with mental focus, intent, and desire being the means, but the processes are similar.

Although, tuning by mental focus is inconsistent and capricious, while electronic tuning is reliable, consistent and tangible, it is no less scientific. The difference being that psychic and medium communication is in its infancy as far as future development goes. It has a scientific basis for its manifestation because all things work according to scientific laws, even though some of these laws haven't been discovered yet.

Consider technology that we now take for granted, such as the television, or microwave. When the former was first developed, there were some who were convinced there were tiny people inside the box acting out scenes! Anyone who would have predicted the things that we now have one hundred years ago would have been scorned and laughed at. So it is with cosmic communication; it is a science in its infancy.

One doesn't have to be practiced in cosmic communication to make contact with what lies beyond, and that includes those from the spirit world. At one time or another, everyone that is alive today has seen them, heard from them, been touched by them, and smelled them, either while in the waking state or through a dream. Those who can't recall having the experience are not aware of the signs or, because of fear and ignorance programmed through religion, are in denial. This is the first step in development of your sixth sense, recognising the times that you have been touched by those in the spirit world.

This hidden power is available to those who recognise and accept that there is a higher realm of knowing and communication beyond their own physical bodies. The universe is full of this unlimited energy that can be tapped by almost anyone who will make the effort to focus and tune themselves to its subtle vibrations. These vibrations are not just for the so-called 'gifted' persons, but for anyone who makes the effort to learn its secrets. Almost all psychic people are so because they recognised the signs of this energy and focused their attention on its workings, which is the very thing that is required in order to develop it. If they hadn't focused their attention on it, then they wouldn't have the 'gifts' they do now.

To begin tuning into this force you need to learn about focusing. Focus on even the smallest instance of psychic phenomena (such as: quantum (spiritual) world, near death experiences, mind reading, clairvoyance, astrology, déjà vu, the quantum field; which is an outcome of the communication of electrons - the worlds of matter and spirit are one and the same) that happens to yourself and to people around you. Play the event around in your mind continually, to get familiar with the sense of the action and presence of the energy involved. This will give you a perception of how involved and integrated is the underlying hidden power that caused the event to take place.

One of the most important things that everyone needs to understand is that every living thing has a consciousness, and is connected to everything other living thing in the universe. People, animals, and plants are all connected to the hidden energy of consciousness that permeates the entire universe and 'wires' all of us together. Understanding and accepting this concept is the most important prerequisite to developing one's own latent ability. The second most important requirement is that the person must have both the desire, and the willingness, to develop and tune themselves so that they can connect with the universal spirit.

After that, it becomes a matter of adopting a certain mindset which is necessary to cultivate a power-thinking process. You will need to diligently practice a number of exercise techniques for feedback while developing these abilities. Feedback helps you recognize and understand the signals and symbols that are received and experienced as a normal part of the learning process. To advance, you need to develop and hone these newfound skills.

Perhaps you can start a circle of your own, although you might risk ridicule if others do not share your beliefs. A circle means weekly meetings where like-minded people can practice in a positive environment.

There you'll begin developing your latent psychic abilities. In addition to these practices, learn to meditate (relax). Although, this is not a rigid requirement, it makes a lot of difference in how fast you progress. You can develop a lot more quickly when you practice meditation.

When you are asleep, so is the physical component of your self. The five senses and your ego, the controlling master, are all temporarily suspended from activity. Sleeping allows the other sense that you have, the sixth sense, to take over for a while without much interference. This is when both the physical body, and your spiritual essence, can perform maintenance simultaneously to help unwrinkle parts of your life. It's ironic that this is the state of being that psychics and mediums practice for years to achieve, and everyone enters it every time they fall asleep.

Those special visits, instructions, lessons and guidance that we receive are sometimes (but not always) interwoven with those mundane dreams your body generates. They are hidden and disguised because you are not supposed to know where the information is coming from. Like it's a big secret.

You are led to believe that you dreamed up all those unique thoughts and ideas all by your little old self. The bad news is that these instructive dreams occur much less frequently than the run-of-the-mill physical dreams. The good news is that when they do happen, the person who has experienced them knows that something special has occurred. Even if they can't figure out what it means, there is a profound sense of purpose or message behind the dream. They become landmarks in many peoples' lives, leaving them with a permanent and unforgettable impression of otherworldliness embedded deep within their subconscious mind. Often for years afterwards, people can remember the most trivial details of those dreams.

Sometimes it is wise to allow your sixth sense to control you. Here is an example: two weeks before his assassination, Abraham Lincoln, the then President of the United States of America, had a dream that there was a funeral at the White House. In the dream he asked a soldier who was in the casket and the reply was, 'The president of United States.' Later when he told his wife about the dream, she remarked that he would die in office.

Could Lincoln have prevented his death? It's possible, had the dream told him how he would die. Then, instead of letting his lone personal bodyguard have the night off, he might have been more concerned about his own safety. However, it's obvious that his death was meant to happen as it did, and that was why his precognitive dream did not give him more information about the circumstances of it.

Another example: Mark Twain had a very realistic dream in which he saw his brother in a casket. He didn't know what to do about it, and so decided to let it go. Less than a week later, his brother was killed in an explosion on a boat. Upon arriving at the town where it took place, he saw his brother laid out in a casket just like in his dream. Again, had the dream given him more specific details about his brother's death, perhaps he could have warned him. The problem is that the laws of nature cannot be challenged with any degree of success. When it's your time to go, there is very little that you can do about it. What is meant to be can only be changed with strenuous, concerted effort.

In both these cases, we have precognitive dreams of the unchangeable kind. They told the future, but without giving enough details for anyone to change the predetermined outcome. Whatever happened, happened because it was already in the universal plan and this cannot be changed.

Then there are the precognitive dreams of the changeable kind. Immediately after the *Titanic* sank in the Atlantic Ocean, there were at least two dozen reports of people who cancelled their trip because of precognitive dreams they had had about the sinking. No one knows how many had the same warning and ignored it, going to a death they could have avoided. One businessman had the same precognitive dream three times, but chose to ignore the warning. He had still intended to make the trip when a sudden turn in business forced him to cancel. Obviously his death was not meant to happen at that time.

The *Titanic* gives a good example of the changeable future. Those few who knew how to interpret their dreams as warnings continued to live. They were given enough details so they could change their future. Those who ignored the warning, or for some reason weren't given one, perished. The businessman is a good example of how an unchangeable future is just that – unchangeable. For in spite of stubbornly ignoring three dream warnings, he was forced to cancel due to a sudden business problem. His future plan required that he remain alive.

These examples should give you some insight into how to view dreams. By giving precognitive dreams more credence, and looking further into them for more precise information, you can benefit from these free glimpses into the future. Whenever you have a dream that seems significant but is unclear, you should be looking for further clarification.

You can get clarification by going back to the source. The next time you are about to fall asleep, think about what type of information you need to clarify the previous dream. Instruct yourself to have a more detailed dream and when it comes, tell yourself that you will awaken. Be sure to have writing material handy. Remember! Don't give up after only one try, keep trying and you'll get something.

The man attributed with inventing the light bulb, Thomas Edison, is said to have done so with the aid of a dream. In fact he used dreams quite a lot for his ideas, and he is not the only one. Dmitry Mendeleyev provided the world of chemistry and physics with the Periodic Table of Elements in 1869. The Table, for which he missed the Nobel Prize in chemistry by one vote, came to him in its completed form in a dream.

Remember that all knowledge already exists in the universe. Infinite quantities of knowledge and information have not yet been transmitted to the minds of humans. Who knows how many other important and mundane discoveries remain to be accessed. We tend to think of future inventions and discoveries, but in reality, these things already exist in the knowledge bank of the universe. It's all a matter of transmission from there to here. You can access this information through your dreams. Solve your personal problems or invent something. Prior to falling asleep, program your mind to access the information presented to you in your dreams. Be persistent and keep trying. It may take time, but you will get a response.

In all three of these cases, the dreamer received help from outside of their subconscious mind's scope of knowledge. Even though they didn't specifically solicit the dream state for the help that they received, they were made the beneficiaries of freely available universal knowledge. But you don't have to wait around for it to be granted to you. Anyone can have the same access if they make the effort to get it. These individuals had experienced a connection to a higher and greater power, and their lives benefited from the encounter. Again, the only requirement is that you actively seek out this information by programming your self to get it while you dream.

I would like to give you my own example of how the sixth sense can work for you. When I started writing this book I thought it would be good to secure a foreword from Noel Edmonds, as it is thanks to him that I owned up to following Cosmic Ordering. I mean, after seeing how the media tore into Tom Cruise for his Scientology beliefs I was not ever going to risk ridicule for something that could have been considered potty.

So, anyway, I sent Noel an email with my request. I didn't want to approach him via his agent as I knew he would be snowed under with similar media requests. I just did it for a bit of fun, and my email went like this:

Dear Noel,

I am writing a book on Cosmic Ordering, I Cosmically Order you to supply me with a foreword for the book.

That was it. I never gave the matter any further thought. At the same time, I was working on placing a TV programme with the title *Godfellas*, which was all about nefarious characters having turned to God. I had been working on placing this for 18 months; I never gave up on it, I always believed in it. About two weeks after I sent the email to Noel I received a telephone call from a Manchester based company, Unique Factuals. They said they had been in talks with ITV1 and that they were interested in commissioning a whole series of these shows. Of course I knew something would happen with it, although I had not placed a Cosmic Order. The reason for my not placing an order was simple. I had work ahead of me that I knew would keep me busy for the next year.

The senior producer at Unique Factuals, Cat Lewis, told me the promising news. I recalled having visited Cat some time prior to receiving her call, probably some 18 months earlier. Although I had bandied the pet project about, I had never really applied a great deal of effort in making it happen. Oh, and who should own Unique Factuals? Who else but … Noel Edmonds! Coincidence? I think not.

Let me tell you, though, what was running through my head when I emailed Noel for that foreword. I had heard that he was a successful businessman with umpteen pokers in the field of TV production. I had toyed with the idea that Noel would come charging through the mist on a white steed, and that he would say, 'Steve, I want to make *Godfellas*.' Where was I when I sent that email? Sitting in front of a fan-driven extractor in the oldest part of my home. Obviously my sixth sense had kicked in and sent a very powerful message out.

I still haven't ordered that this TV programme go ahead, but every single person I have approached with the request to appear in each of the possible 12 documentaries have all said 'yes'. The characters range from an ex-Triad gang member turned Methodist minister to an ex-Kray gang member turned Born Again Christian. I have succeeded in securing 20 characters, all with chequered pasts, to appear, and not all are of Christian belief, as I believe religion to be universal.

So the next time you have a feeling of impending doom, listen to it. Equally so, once you activate your sixth sense, you can make good things come about, as I have shown you in some of the previous examples.

Remember, always put something back into the universe by means of an acknowledgment, and say 'thank you' for what you have been granted.

15

My Rags to Riches Story

My only regret in life is not having given a down-and-out the price of a cup of a tea. I was 17, walking home from work, when a rough-looking man with worn out clothes asked me for the price of a cup of tea. I brusquely walked past him, but after a few steps, something in my head told me to give him the handful of coins I had in my pocket. I stopped, and looked around, but he was gone. I actually felt shudderings of regret in my soul.

No surprisingly, I now always put my hand in my pocket when I see a street vendor selling *The Big Issue*, a UK magazine sold by homeless people, giving them a chance to earn a legitimate income. I also find myself giving to every down-and-out I come across in the hope that I can find the one I denied when I was 17. When I go to London's King's Cross Station by train, I usually end up tipping my pockets of loose change out to street beggars, trying to buy back a lost chance that haunts me. I would not call myself a philanthropist, by any means, but I do my own little things, in my own way.

Not surprisingly, my first appeal to the universe, back in the Nineties, fell on deaf ears. My 'requests' were actually self-centred demands, full of anger. I suppose, coming from someone who did not like themselves, this was to be expected, but it did not enamour me to the cosmos. My trip to the library brought me a step closer to learning what love and harmony were all about. I cannot even recall the names of some of those early books I borrowed about philosophy and the like, but that is when I discovered how to empty myself of anger and pretence.

I have to admit that, in order to cover up my lack of cash, I had stooped to lying. Of course, in my mind, I knew I would never be able to find the money for rent, or for the big fancy presents I had promised my friends. I was living in a fantasy world, and I hated myself for not being who I said I was. My little Iranian friend and I would spend hours in deep conversation, often struggling to find the words to express what we meant. In terms of worldly goods, I had nothing of value. No money in the bank and only a hard luck story to send me to sleep at nights.

With perseverance, I eventually managed to find the Holy Grail of keys to unlock what my little Iranian friend was trying to convey to me. I ditched the old me, and started to uncover some of the revelations of the mystical universe. It was the same sort of thing as the hippies of the Sixties were once pushing, but I left out the 'peace to you, man' bit, and discovered that what you did for the good of others came back to reward you.

I started to give more of my time to non-religious voluntary causes. I would drive elderly people around in a battered Community Transport bus for no greater a reward than a homemade curry. This meal would be served up to me by a commune of hippies, well past their 'sell by' date. The hippies who ran the charity-based service seemed to run on fresh air. I don't know if it was coincidence or what, but I saw a lot of my Iranian friend's teachings come to life while doing this voluntary work. I began reading about all sorts of things.

Certainly, the stories of aliens coming from another planet, and the romantic notion that we might have descended from a higher order, gave me the impetus to look deeper into how mankind was once able to achieve things that now seem almost impossible. I recall how my quest for reason was, at times, like climbing a greasy pole. My blurred inner vision often gelled fact and fiction into one. In my Don Quixote-type quest, I stumbled before I could walk, and I staggered before I could run. Before long, I was led by a combination of things to look to the universe for fulfilment. Finally, one night, it came to me …

I was parked near the sea. It was a winter's night, and the sky was awash with twinkling stars, each sending out its own message of hope. As ludicrous as it may seem, I was in awe at what was up there. Up until then, I had not really bothered about such matters. Until then, I would have been the first to call anyone looking up at the stars in such amazement a buffoon. But from thereon everything just seemed to slot together beautifully.

My impatience and anger at being unable to suddenly manifest wealth subsided, and I knew for certain that I would eventually become wealthy. I did not have one shred of doubt that it would happen, though I hardly had any money at all. Little by little, I built up my portfolio of life's achievements. I wanted to be in charge of my own destiny, not to have my thoughts corrupted by power-crazed political and religious leaders.

After I had found myself, the biggest thought I could muster was 'I want a place to call my own, and a warm pillow to put my head down on every night'. At first, I wasn't even sure if that was too much to ask for. I lacked confidence, and was self-conscious about what I was doing. But, in time, it became second nature, and I started to see results.

Prior to this, in a vain attempt to line my pockets, I used to gamble on the horses. In response to adverts in the *Racing Post*, I would send my hard-earned cash to buy what is called 'insider information'. Often, more times than I care to remember, the information was duff and I would go on to a different system, even picking my own losers.

This time, though, I felt different. I knew that it was the law of the universe that governed the horses, not tipsters; you could not go against nature. Armed with my newfound belief, I walked into Ladbrokes betting shop with the intention of coming out a winner. The night before I had asked the universe to guide me in what I was doing, so I knew for certain that what I was going to do would produce results.

What I am going to tell you now is rather embarrassing. In fact, I am sure you will all see why I have kept this revelation locked away within me for over ten years. Well, at the risk of being branded mad, here I go. I asked the cosmos to be able to connect with the horses, to get them to tell me which one of them had the power and energy to win. I wanted my senses to be heightened so that I would be able to read the signs of a winner. I know it sounds crazy, and if not for Noel Edmonds coming out with how the cosmos helped him restart his TV career, I would have continued to keep all of this to myself.

Studying the horses on the TV screen in the betting shop preceded my first bet. I was looking for a sign, anything. I remember repeatedly saying in my mind, 'Give me a sign'. One of the horses kept twitching its ear. Maybe it was a sign, or maybe it was a fly, or just the horse's nerves. I then asked if that particular horse twitching its ear was the sign, and the horse nodded its head up and down!

As I wrote out the betting slip I looked around in a self-conscious way, to see if people around me were looking at me funny. I cannot even remember the name of that horse, nor have I a copy of that first winning betting slip, which I wish now that I had kept. The horse that had nodded to me romped home in first place, and I collected my winnings, just as I had envisioned myself doing.

Again, I placed another £10 bet, and that horse won. I had to leave the betting shop as my heart was racing so fast. When I arrived home, my fingers trembled as I counted out my winnings, over £100!

Sometimes I would get it wrong. Maybe the horse really did have a fly in its ear, or it was genuinely nervous. However, I was soon able to discern the signals from the winning horse with greater accuracy. Sometimes there would be no signal. I now put that down to how full the betting shop was. All those other punters putting out too much energy into the place must have been blocking my own.

I always stood back from the rows of TV monitors, as this was something I knew would cause a connection to be lost, with no signs of normal service being resumed for a while.

I remember one time, visiting the betting shop every day for over a week without any signs, but I never wavered from my belief. The signs were not always the same; sometimes it was the jockey giving the sign, or one horse pointing to another one that was going to win. Sometimes it would be a sort of premonition, I would look at the names of the runners in the press and something would stand out, that was the horse.

I would hold the paper out in front of me and stare at it, letting my mind empty. I never let a horse's name influence me. I am not advocating gambling, in fact I would advise against it, as you have to have an unwavering belief before contemplating such a thing.

As I write this I feel self-conscious that someone is going to put me down as a loon. As far as I am aware, I am absolutely sane. I do not take drugs, I am not an alcoholic, and am not on prescribed drugs or medication. I am sure my friends and associates would vouch for my sanity, although perhaps not after they read this ...

Sometimes I would believe a race to be fixed, because a lot of the horses would be on edge, and they would send mixed signals. There would be a few horses giving me the signal; perhaps one was the theoretical winner that would not be first past the post, and the other giving the signal would be the fixed winner. And maybe the other horses were warning me not to bet. I just had that feeling.

Then there was the race that was not on the closed circuit TV system used by Ladbrokes, it would come through the speakers into the shop. I would listen intently for a sign, as, of course, the horse could not signal. After some intense effort, I could pick out little sounds that would signify the winner. These non-televised races would see my stakes lowered, as I was beginning to hear things that were not real.

Sometimes I felt the compulsion to tell someone about what I was doing, or I felt I would burst. But fear of being branded mad stopped me from doing so. I also thought that if I told anyone about what was happening, then my winning streak would stop. Perhaps I might anger the universe by telling people. Now, of course, I know that this is not the case. The more people you have rooting for you, the better chance you have of success.

I know this may all come across as far-fetched, and even as I write this, I too find it hard to tell of what went on. Yet, I feel an unwavering period of belief coming over me as well. I am not worried if the sceptic says I am mad, as I know it happened. I am not going to turn water into wine just to appease the sceptics.

My stakes on the races varied depending on my mood. I did not want to seem greedy, but at times I couldn't help myself. Soon I had great difficulty in getting the clerks on the betting windows in Ladbrokes to give me the odds. Say the horse was priced at 10/1, I might ask to 'take the odds'. Of course if I were putting £500 on the horse then the clerk would have to tell the betting shop manager, and he or she would have to call head office for permission to take the bet. Usually, by the time they got back to me, the race had nearly started and the odds had, miraculously, dropped to something like 5/1. All that I can say is that I may have been too greedy and perhaps the universe was giving me a telling off.

In all, over a period of a few months, I won over £25,000. I reproduce some of the winning betting slips herein, which I started to photocopy before handing the originals in to the payout clerk. I did not know why I was doing it back then, but something inside me told me to. Now I know why! As you will see, they all bear the

Ladbrokes header and all are coded in the Ladbrokes automated coding system, I cannot fake them. Even if I could, I know I would be holding myself open to criminal charges if they were forgeries.

Standing in a betting shop is a tiresome business, especially when you do not get any signals for a few weeks. After winning so much money, I began to feel a bit guilty. I felt I should put something back into the universe so that others could benefit from it. I had already secured two small business ventures which gave me a regular income. This came about after I changed my ways, I requested that my new ways be put to industrious use … and sure enough they were.

My first business was in the service industry. I won a half-share in the company by convincing the owner that I would increase turnover tenfold, which I knew I could. I requested of the cosmos that the industrious people around me who wanted to earn money should get it, as they deserved it. So I started employing some of these industrious people. I was happy for them to earn more money, as were they.

Soon after this I opened my own business. I had asked the cosmos to allow me to unlock my hidden talents, and sure enough it happened. I had changed from demanding £1 million be posted through my letterbox, to making more reasonable requests. I suppose it would have been good to have a cheque for £1 million turn up on my front doormat one morning, but in reality requests have to be put in context.

Yes, I believe that a cheque for £1 million will eventually turn up, I do not doubt it. However, no one in his or her right mind can make such a feat happen from nothing. There has to be an action to bring it about, which is what I want you to understand. You have to be realistic. There is much more likelihood of £10,000 turning up on your doormat in cheque form, because of all the millions of possible ways this could come about. If you are poor, there is not much chance of a £1 million cheque manifesting itself in front of you, but the overall fulfilment of that request can still come about, if you really want it to happen. It just may take some time.

You have to start the ball rolling, get things working, feel lucky, and know that something positive is going to happen. Feel worthy of your requests. Always look to put something back into the universe. This can be in the form of small services to others, even just one small action per day. It does not have to be anything dramatic or hugely philanthropic.

I do not go around looking for moments when I can repay some of the kindness shown to me by the cosmos, they just turn up. Sometimes it is just in the form of a friendly smile. I am always surprised at the number of people who walk around with their heads down, afraid of meeting another's gaze. I often end up smiling at the top of someone's tilted head, and I laugh to myself.

I endured a pretty tough upbringing, so I feel the need to help those less fortunate than myself. I asked the cosmos for my knowledge to be increased, and that it be used to help people. Sure enough it has happened. Out of the blue, I saw an advert about becoming a counsellor. After qualifying, I went on to help numerous people. Perhaps I was even a little overly helpful at times. I always knew when this had happened, as the cosmos would tell me with a sign. Soon after, I qualified as a clinical hypnotherapist, and then I really set about helping people. The rewards were larger than I ever thought possible, and I thanked the cosmos.

Soon I was curing people of all sorts of hang-ups, fears, phobias, sexual problems, addictions, etc, etc. But eventually I began to feel a bit hemmed-in. I wanted to help even more people. So I asked the cosmos for my talents to be used to reach thousands of people, and I took up writing. This came about in a very weird way. I had no intentions of writing a book, although I had written some very sorry-looking booklets with absorbing titles: *Forever Young, How to Win the Lottery*, etc, etc. This was something I dabbled in after asking the cosmos to reveal my hidden talents. I even designed a potion that would keep you young looking, and it works.

I had the subject for a true crime book in mind, but I just did not have the confidence to write a book. I mean, it was all very well asking the cosmos to allow my senses to be heightened so I could do marvellous things at the bookies, but to me writing a book was something only Stephen King and the likes could do.

I phoned around some of the local universities, calling their English Literature departments to see if anyone could help me write this particular book. Each time, I was fobbed off to other departments, or told to phone some other person. After a full afternoon of getting nowhere, I came to the conclusion that universities were full of not-very-helpful people. Perhaps this is true, but I do know that it was also the doing of the cosmos. Eventually, I sat down and strung some words together and wrote my first book.

Not once did I think of going to a mainstream publisher with my manuscript. I started my own company, the imprint of Mirage Publishing. I was as naïve as could be, which turned out to be a good thing. Had I known what running a publishing house entailed, then I would have thought the cosmos had gone stark raving mad. It was certainly a bigger challenge than I had ever thought I could handle.

Again, I owed the cosmos a great big thank you. I did this with my writing style, which was what the Americans call 'live writing'. It entails leaving all the errors in the text, as they have subliminal meanings, and not editing your first draft … that is how different I was. My early books were lavish with my live writing style, but now I conform due to the fact that many people who read my first lot of books believed I was illiterate.

Some time later, Mirage Publishing produced its first title, and within months all stock had sold out. I thanked the cosmos. Two things had happened at once: my request that my talents be given a new area of work; and that I would reach thousands of people.

I could go on to document how my requests to the cosmos have been granted, but that would take up a whole book of its own. I have already written about the main ones in here. There have been some very private requests that have also been granted to me, and I thank the cosmos for those as well.

Oh, I do have one remarkable thing to relate to you. I asked the cosmos for my friendship to be reciprocated by someone who would give as much back to me as I gave to them. I referred to my friend's suicide, and how much I longed to share my friendship with another as much as I had with him.

I said, 'Oh great Oneness of the universe, I am a very good person to be someone's best friend. I have so much warmth within me that I know someone will benefit from that. All I ask is that I be allowed to trust in them, and be able to confide my feelings without them laughing at me when I do so. I do not care what they look like or what they do. I know that by having a best buddy that I will have someone who will not let me down, and I will not let them down.'

A little while after this, a friend of mine was moving from a house to a tower block. He had a little dog, a Yorkshire terrier that was 11 months old. The problem was that pets were not allowed in the tower block. The terrier's name was Harley.

I took Harley in, as I couldn't bear to see him go to a cat and dog shelter, although I never intended to keep him.

I was in a quandary, stuck with a terrier. I advertised in the free-ads newspaper: 'Free to good home, a Yorkshire terrier …'. A week later the ad appeared, but by then Harley had grown on me.

The phone rang soon after, 'Hello, is the Yorkshire Terrier still available?' the person on the other end of the line asked.

'No, it's gone I'm afraid,' I replied as I sat with Harley on my lap.

Call me soft or whatever, but I couldn't give Harley up. Now all these years later, I have a friend I can confide my feelings to without them laughing at me, and someone I can share my friendship with. Little Harley understands a lot of words, he's a great, loyal friend and comes almost everywhere with me. I have even sneaked him into hotel rooms. He stands in a holdall, with his little nose poking out of the end, where I leave the zipper open a little way to give him air. He is a clever little fellow, and knows not to say anything when in that holdall. Of course, when in bed and people walk past the hotel room, he gives the game away by giving a gruff warning bark. His protective warning awakens me, and I cuddle him in. Soon he goes back to sleep, lying on his back with his head on the pillow! I thanked the cosmos then for my new friend, and I still do so today.

The last ten years have been such a turnaround from the days when I could not even afford a can of dog food. Now I control my own destiny. I have written nearly 40 non-fiction books, directed a video documentary, and I regularly supply news stories to national newspapers throughout the UK. None of these things have happened by chance, that is for sure.

I have written numerous books relating to true crime, but in return for this cosmic gift I felt it only fair that victims of crime be given a chance to heal their mental scars, and that something be put back into the universe that would help others. I asked the cosmos to direct my writing skills to helping victims of crime. Soon after that I worked with Caroline Roberts, a surviving victim of the notorious UK killing couple, Fred and Rose West. I have also worked with Hailey Giblin, a surviving victim of UK double-child killer Ian Huntley. The cosmos granted my request, for which I thanked it.

Just as a particular petroleum company uses the slogan 'The Lion Goes from Strength to Strength', it seems that I am doing the same in my life, thanks to the cosmos. I have had books serialised in numerous daily and Sunday newspapers throughout the UK. I might put one book being serialised down to chance and good luck, but not seven! My books have also featured in numerous national magazines, even serialised in them.

I do not believe that all of the good that has happened to me is down to chance or luck. My life used to be hell. I was the typical sceptic. I still almost cannot believe that my life has been turned around so drastically, and in such a short space of time. I know that my expectations have become higher, and as a consequence so have my requests to the cosmos, on par with my current lifestyle. But I still know that these requests will be fulfilled.

I do not want to sound pompous, or to keep blowing my own trumpet. I just want to show you what has happened to me – all as a direct result of Cosmic Ordering. Do not wait for something to happen; make it happen now. Just remember that for everything you take out of the universe, you should put something back into it. Every day I make sure to help someone, even in a small way. Do not let the deficit build up, as the cosmos will not be happy with you.

I would like to think that you, too, now have an unwavering belief in yourself. I hope my rags to riches story, and this guide, will inspire you. Good luck.

16

Cosmic Winnings

In this final chapter I have chosen a random selection of winning betting slips from 1996, all written in my own hand, and all genuine. Some you will see, if you can read the dates and times, that they do match up to my claims. I give this guarantee, that if they are found to be forgeries or are found not to be copies of some of my winning betting slips then I hold myself open to criminal proceedings for passing fakes off as genuine articles.

Some are timed as having had the bet placed a short while before the race started, some earlier. The dates are from February through to June 1996. Some slips have more than one horse listed, from memory I cannot recall if all on the slip won, but if they did not then I have already stated the possible reasons as to why the horse did not win.

Over a period of months I amassed over £25,000 in winnings. Of course, standing around in a betting shop is a boring business, especially if you are not receiving any signals. I believe I had a silent period of two weeks in duration, but I persevered. I am not advocating gambling, in fact I have given it up due to how greedy I was becoming. Remember, you cannot keep taking without giving something back in return. I much prefer to help others, as I would hope you, too, would.

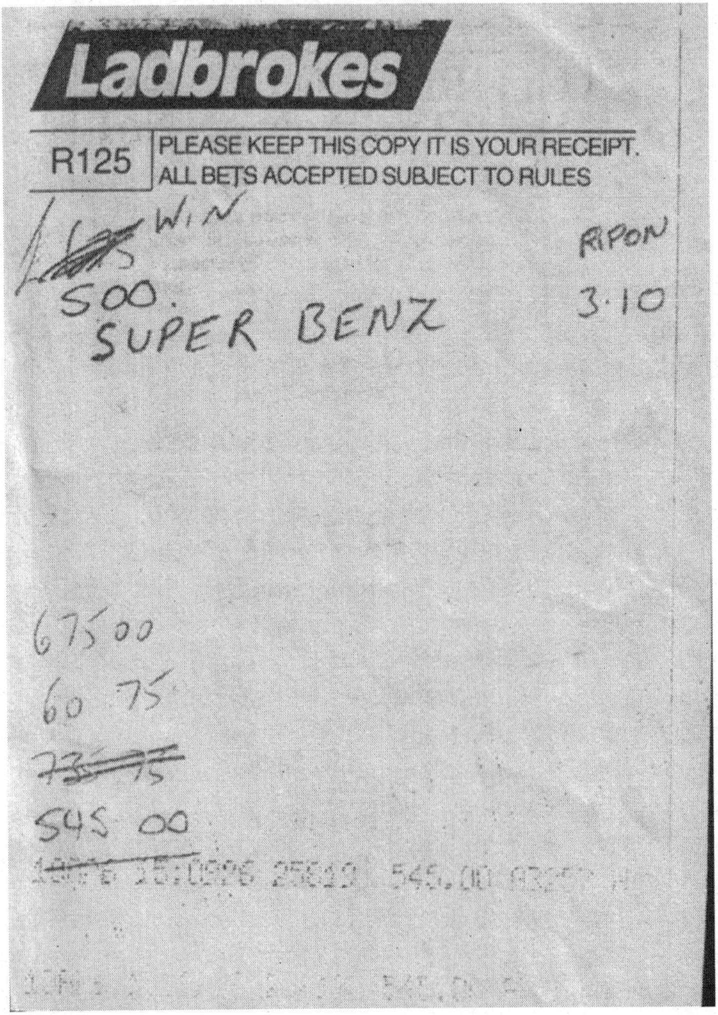

Ladbrokes

R125 PLEASE KEEP THIS COPY IT IS YOUR RECEIPT.
ALL BETS ACCEPTED SUBJECT TO RULES

WIN

RIPON

500.

3.10

SUPER BENZ

675 00

60 75

545 00

Ladbrokes

| R55 | PLEASE KEEP THIS COPY IT IS YOUR RECEIPT. ALL BETS ACCEPTED SUBJECT TO RULES |

£535 WIN HIGHLAND WAY   2.30
                            HEXHAM

£535 WIN SOURCE OF LIGHT   3.40
                            NOTTINGHAM

107000
963 0
1166 30

22APR 53:3108 29767 1166.30 R3257 HTH

22APR 13:3108 29767 1166.30 R3257 HTH

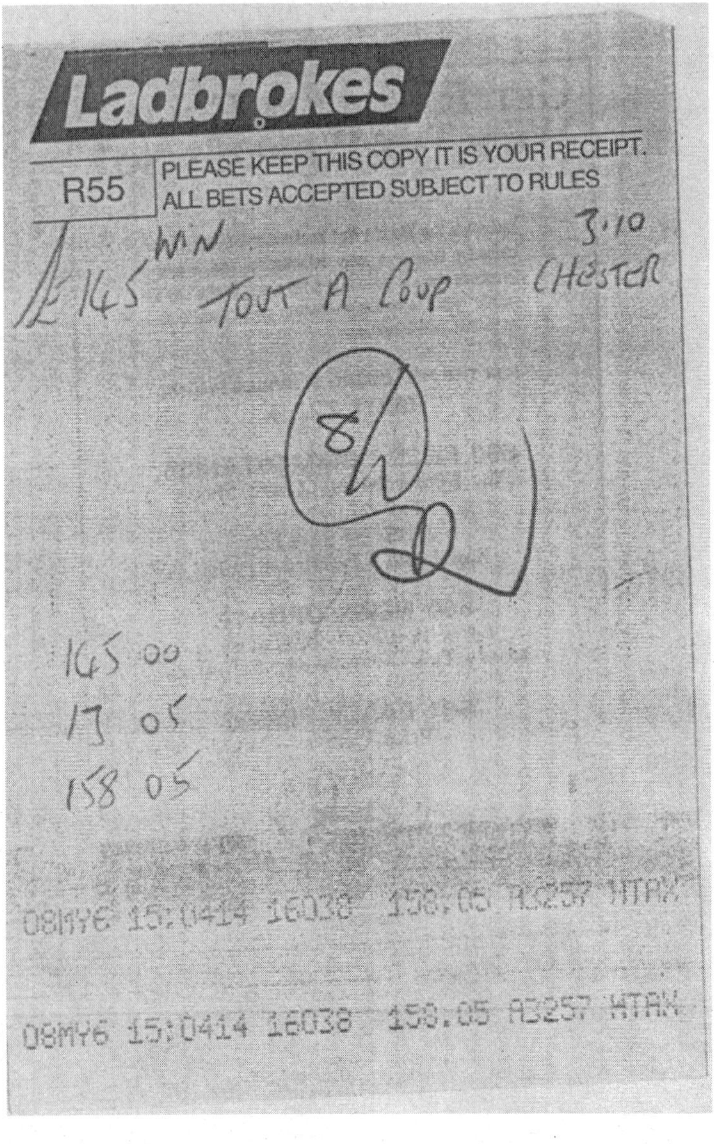
Ladbrokes
R55
PLEASE KEEP THIS COPY IT IS YOUR RECEIPT.
ALL BETS ACCEPTED SUBJECT TO RULES
WIN
3.10
£145 TOUT A COUP CHESTER
8/1
145 00
17 05
158 05
08MY6 15:0414 16038 158.05 A3257 HTAX
08MY6 15:0414 16038 158.05 A3257 HTAX

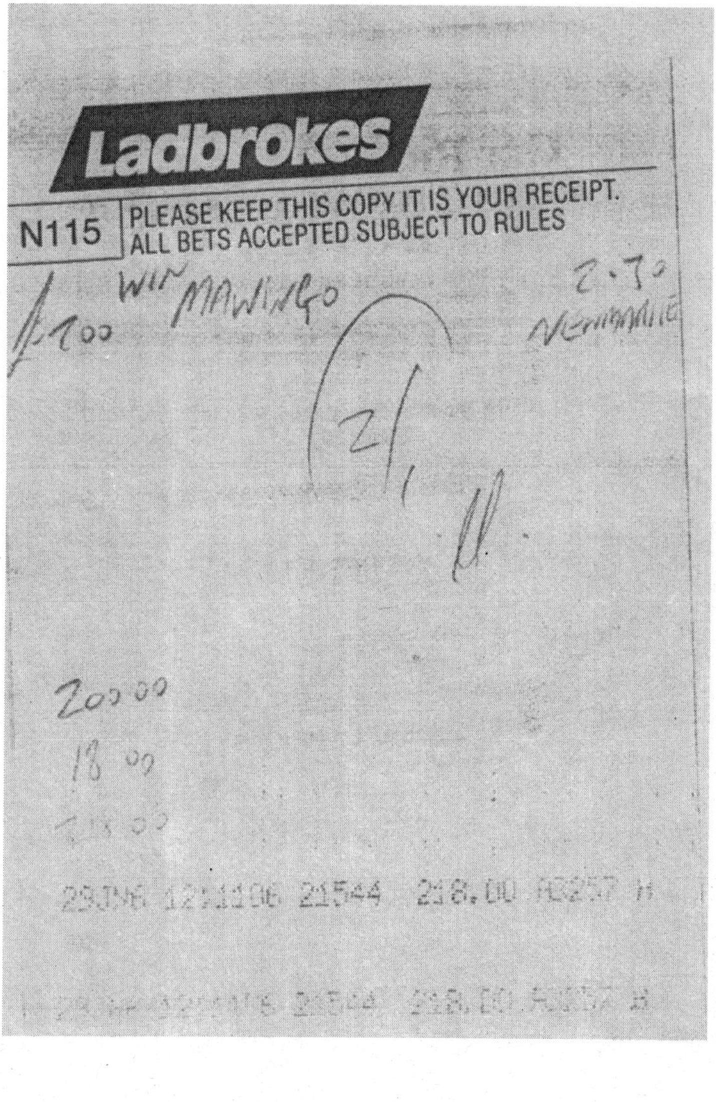

Ladbrokes

N115 PLEASE KEEP THIS COPY IT IS YOUR RECEIPT.
ALL BETS ACCEPTED SUBJECT TO RULES

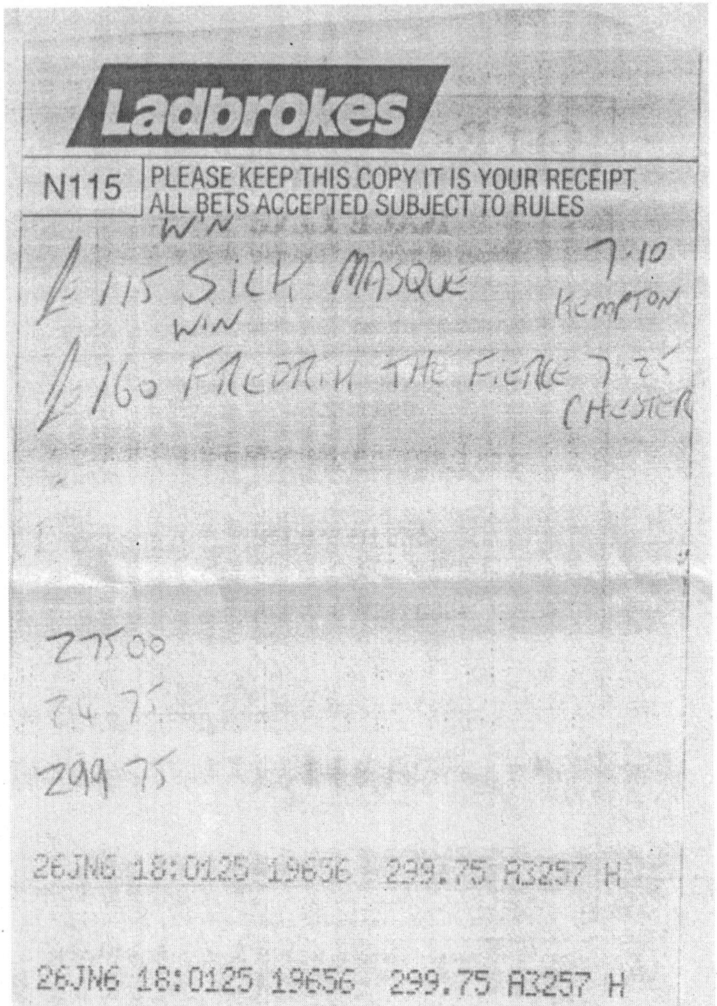

Ladbrokes

N115 PLEASE KEEP THIS COPY IT IS YOUR RECEIPT
ALL BETS ACCEPTED SUBJECT TO RULES

WIN
£115 SICK MASQUE 7.10
KEMPTON
WIN
£160 FREDRICK THE FIERCE 7.25
CHESTER

27500
24 75
299 75

26JN6 18:0125 19656 299.75 A3257 H

26JN6 18:0125 19656 299.75 A3257 H

Ladbrokes

| R125 | PLEASE KEEP THIS COPY IT IS YOUR RECEIPT. ALL BETS ACCEPTED SUBJECT TO RULES |

£5 WIN SHARP 'N SMART — LINGFIELD 4·05

£5 WIN RIGHTEOUS GENT — LINGFIELD 4·35

104 00

10·40

114 40

10838067 1.56 *114.40

Ladbrokes

R55 | PLEASE KEEP THIS COPY IT IS YOUR RECEIPT.
ALL BETS ACCEPTED SUBJECT TO RULES

£ 190 WIN VASARI   2·40
CH.SLT

190 00
17.10
207 10

08MY6 14:0438 15957 207.10 A3257 HTAX

08MY6 14:0438 15957 207.10 A3257 HTAX

COSMIC ORDERING COURSE

Quite a few devotees of Cosmic Ordering have asked about courses. Prompted by the overwhelming amount of requests, Stephen Richards has indicated that he would be willing to lead some weekend courses if there was sufficient interest.

For more details see the website
www.cosmicordering.net

Other Titles by this Publisher

*Burnt: Surviving Against all the Odds – Beaten, Burnt and Left for Dead.
One Man's Inspiring Story of His Survival After Losing His Legs*
Ian Colquhoun
Cosmic Ordering Connection
Stephen Richards
Cosmic Ordering Guide
Stephen Richards
Cosmic Ordering Healing Oracle Cards
Stephen Richards
Cosmic Ordering: Oracle Wish Cards
Stephen Richards & Karen Whitelaw Smith
Cosmic Ordering Service: 101 Orders For Daily Use
Stephen Richards
The Butterfly Experience: Inspiration For Change
Karen Whitelaw Smith
*The Tumbler: A 16-year-old Boy's Live Chronicle of Auschwitz, Belsen,
Hanover, Hildesheim, Wolgsberg and Wüstegiersdorf Nazi Death Camps*
Azriel Feuerstein
Past Life Tourism
Barbara Ford-Hammond
*The Real Office: An Uncharacteristic Gesture of Magnanimity
by Management Supremo Hilary Wilson-Savage*
Hilary Wilson-Savage

Prospective Titles
*Cosmic Ordering - Chakra Clearing for a Better
Connection: Oracle Cards*
Stephen Richards
Internet Dating
Clive Worth
Life Without Lottie
Fiona Fridd
Mrs Darley's Pagan Whispers
Carole Carlton
*Occult: The Psychic Jungle - Satanic Cults, Voodoo Killings and Conspiracy
Theories Uncovered by Investigative Author*
Jonathan Charles Tapsell

Mirage Publishing Website:
www.miragepublishing.com

Submissions of Mind, Body & Spirit manuscripts welcomed from new authors.